TRAVELING LIGHT

PAT McGEACHY

Nashville   ABINGDON PRESS   New York

TRAVELING LIGHT

Copyright © 1975 by Abingdon Press

Library of Congress Cataloging in Publication Data

McGeachy, Pat
  Traveling Light.
  1. Stewardship, Christian. I. Title.
BV772.M3514   248'.6   75-17572

ISBN 0-687-42530-1

.

Scripture quotations are from the Revised Standard Version of the Bible, copyrighted 1946, 1952, and 1971 by the Division of Christian Education, National Council of Churches, and are used by permission.

MANUFACTURED BY THE PARTHENON PRESS AT NASHVILLE, TENNESSEE, UNITED STATES OF AMERICA

CONTENTS

I THE THING IS . . .

Things.

Thing is such an ordinary word that we assume that everyone knows what it means. So it can mean most anything:

"Did you wash the breakfast things?"

"Doing my thing."

"I've got a thing about you, baby."

"The thing about politics is compromise."

"She is a foolish, foolish thing."

In short, things are not always what they seem.

So, when we say *thing* in this book, let's say we'll usually mean "material thing," as distinct from "person" or "spirit."

There sure are a lot of things! Not even a hermit can escape them: in addition to his cave and his soup he is surrounded by rocks, trees, stars, air, insects.

Where do they all come from? (Have you ever suspected that coat hangers multiply in the closet at night?) Sometimes, after dealing with a stubborn lawn mower, the five o'clock traffic, or my unbalanced budget, I almost feel that things are out to get me. But that can't be—for I too am a thing. Like the rocks and trees, I am a created being made of molecules and atoms.

Things are all around, and even within me. And yet, I have been taught as a Christian that somehow I and my fellow human beings stand apart from the created order. This mystery has been known ever since the Bible's hymnbook sang:

> What is man that thou art mindful of him . . .?
> Yet thou hast made him little less than God (Ps. 8:4-5).

We are not simply part of the created order, but have been given responsibility over it (Ps. 8:6) and instructed to use it wisely and well, both for joy and duty (Gen. 1:28-30). We are at once part of the world of things, and in charge of it. It is both a privilege and a problem.

When we begin to age, or are seriously ill, or a loved one dies, our *thingness* becomes very real. We feel like a machine out of order, or running down, and we are very mortal, disposable, useless. When there's an energy crisis, we all feel insecure. Restocking the old fallout shelter can give us a momentary sense of security, but it is an illusion. We are like the rich fool in Jesus' story who stored all his things and said, "Take your ease, eat, drink, and be merry." When you wish for tomorrow's paper, to see if you have struck it rich on the stock market, remember, you could find your name in the obituary column.

When we put trust in things, we make gods of them, just as surely as Isaiah's ridiculous lumberman: "He chooses a holm tree . . . and lets it grow strong . . . Then it becomes fuel for a man; he takes a part of it and warms himself, he kindles a fire and bakes bread; also he makes a god and worships it" (44:14-15). Such gods do not possess the power to help, obviously. What is not so obvious is that they *do* possess the power to destroy. False gods cannot save, but they can enslave:

A man finds himself working day and night to the point of exhaustion, or even death, to support a life-style for his family that they do not need.

A woman feels miserable, unhappy, and out of place because she cannot afford the latest fashions; her wardrobe means so much to her that she cannot be at ease around her friends who are dressed "acceptably."

A boy spends all his waking hours dreaming of a motorcycle, believing that if he only had one, he would be happy.

A daughter begrudges every dime she must spend to take care of her aged and helpless mother, so the two of them never have fun together any more.

This could be an endless list. But they would all sound the same, and in the end they would lead to something like the following stories, both true:

Soldiers crossing war-torn France found a woman in the ruins of her cottage, beside her dead cow, saying, *"Le bon Dieu, il est mort"* (God is dead).

An American teenager holds in her hand the steering knob of her wrecked sports car, and cries to her minister, "There's your God—what's left of him!"

Well, what would *your* reaction be if you suddenly lost everything? Do you trust God, or the things God has made? Do you think you would respond like the woman who answered the radio interviewer after the recent tornadoes swept mid-America:

Reporter: *What were you thinking of while the wind was snatching away your house?*

Woman: *Nothing much. I was too busy praying.*

Reporter: *Well, now that it's over, what are you thinking?*

Woman: Just thanking God that none of us was hurt.

In some ways the loss of all things can be a liberating experience. Once I lost my calendar with all my appointments for the month. First I panicked: "How will I know what to do next?" But then I felt a great sense of liberation: "I'm free! I don't have to do anything!" (Darn it, I found the thing shortly thereafter!)

As I am writing this, the world is emerging from a winter-long fuel shortage. A very wise man said to me, "Too bad it wasn't a lot worse." "Why?" I asked in some surprise. "Because we need to walk more," he answered. "And because we need to learn again something that we have forgotten: *Things were not made to last forever.*" There is a limit to the natural resources of the earth. Listen to the haunting story of the disappearance of the most beautiful tree in eastern America, told by Donald Culross Peattie:

Much of Pennsylvania and almost all of New York outside the Adirondacks . . . was one vast White Pine forest. Pioneers used to say that a squirrel could travel a squirrel's lifetime without ever coming down out of the White Pines, and save for the intersection of rivers this may have been but slight hyperbole. When the male flowers bloomed in these illimitable pineries, thousands of miles of forest aisle were swept with the golden smoke of the reckless fertility, and great storms of pollen were swept from the primeval shores far out to sea and to the superstitious sailor seemed to be "raining brimstone" on the deck.

Nor can one conceive, from the second growth that is almost all that is left to us, of the topping height of the virgin White Pines. Trees 150 feet tall astounded the first settlers and explorers; eighty feet or more of the trunk of such a specimen might be free of branches, marvelously thick and straight. On the present site of Dartmouth College, a specimen 240 feet in

10

height was measured. This would surpass anything in the eastern United States, and would do credit to Douglas Fir of the West, and even the Redwood. Similar heights were recorded from Maine, Quebec and . . . New York, in pioneering times. How many others fell unmeasured or unrecorded, we cannot know.[1]

No one could believe that this rich storehouse of masts, paneling, shingles, matches, window frames, and siding would ever be depleted. But one day the nation woke to find its treasure gone. "Though public opinion came too late to save the virgin White Pine, it made itself felt just in time to save the great forests of the Western States, to back Theodore Roosevelt and the Forest Service and National Parks in their battle for Conservation."[2]

Perhaps the current energy crisis can be interpreted as the voice of God, calling as of old for us to tend the garden in which he has placed us, and warning that our resources are being depleted. Not everyone believes this. In May, 1974, the Presbyterian Outlook quoted the United Church of Canada's Department of Church and Society, saying: "Let's not be pessimistic. Let us remember that man is greater than his environment, and, given thought, can control and change it."

But can we? Whether we look at the problem of the world's resources or our own family budgets, we begin to wonder if we really are in charge or if it is as Emerson said, "Things are in the saddle and ride mankind."

One of our problems is our remarkable education! The advance of science has both soothed and upset us. So

[1]*A Natural History of Trees* (New York: Bonanza Books, 1966), pp. 4-6.
[2]*Ibid.*, p. 14.

11

many wonderful inventions have been discovered that we have been lulled into false security. Very few people die of appendicitis or pneumonia any more; only cancer and the circulatory diseases remain the great killers, and even they are being brought under control by radiation, transplants, open-heart surgery, and chemotherapy. The word "plague" which struck terror into medieval Europe, is heard rarely in our streets. Once C. S. Lewis' wife asked a friend whether she had ever thought of death, and was told, "By the time I reach that age, science will have done something about it."[3] She needed to read Luke 12:20: "Fool! This night your soul is required of you."

Yes. But if science's advance has helped us forget our frailty, it has also called attention to it. Since 1946 every child born has lived with the shadow of nuclear destruction. And as space travel and modern astronomy open the doors to infinity, we become aware that we are small creatures, on an insignificant galaxy, in a sky filled with monstrous things: quasars, pulsars, black holes. Yeats was right: "Things fall apart; the center cannot hold." The world is frightening, huge, ominous, and impersonal. And it doesn't manage very well.

You know all that, if you've ever tried to get a coat hanger out of a hall closet, or balance a budget. "Mind doesn't matter, for matter won't mind." But what do Christians do with a world which won't be managed, when we are under orders to subdue it (Gen. 1:28)? Throughout the Old Testament we have marching instructions to earth's wayfaring strangers: "Build

[3]C. S. Lewis, God in the Dock (Grand Rapids, Mich: William B. Eerdmans, 1970), p. 226.

houses and live in them; plant gardens and eat their produce. Take wives and have sons and daughters" (Jer. 29:5-6). We may not like it, but we live in the world of things, and we need a philosophy to live by. We need, I submit, a kind of *Christian materialism* that will not neglect our responsibility toward things, but at the same time will not take them too seriously.

And we can get it from Jesus, who loved things, but would not grant them ultimate importance. Side by side (in the Sermon on the Mount) with our Lord's talk of the kingdom of heaven, we find earthy words: hunger, thirst, salt, light, gift, judge, prison, penny, lust, hand, hair, eye, tooth, cheek, coat, cloak, sun, rain, taxes, alms, closet, door, moth, rust, thieves, treasure. But he cautions us not to worship these things. We are to appreciate the world, but not to confuse it with the kingdom of heaven. Gentiles and tax collectors may look for creature comforts, but the person of faith, like the birds and flowers, must not worry about them. Rather, Jesus said, "Seek first his kingdom and his righteousness, and all these things shall be yours as well" (Matt. 6:33).

Jesus' strong earthy words were translated into a strong earthy life. See him now: going through thirst and hunger, in the dust of the Palestinian roads, munching grain in a field, breaking loaves and fish with a crowd, touching lepers, and calling to people not to follow him for the food he brings (John 6:26-27). He does not seek material gain, but refuses the devil's taunt to turn stones into bread (Luke 4:3-4). Look well at him, he is a strange figure—a king born in a stable, a philosopher who never wrote a book, an evangelist who seemed to run from crowds, a leader who told people not to follow him. He ordered us not to worry about things, and yet he loved them, and peppered his speech with the words of a carpenter, or man of the soil: flowers, birds, fish, bread, log, dogs, pearls, wolves, sheep, grapes, thorns, thistles, rock.

This is our Lord, who loved nature, but called us not to lay up treasure upon earth. What are we to make of him? If we become ascetics in monasteries, how can we fulfill the responsibility that he has given us? (Remember that the ten-talent servant was rewarded for his industry, Matt. 25:14-30.) On the other hand, if, in the tradition of the American work ethic, we get ahead and become good stewards of much property, how can we justify such great possession when there are so many hungry people in the world?

It is not an easy question. It may be life's toughest. And every condominium advertisement is an attempt to handle it:

FIND TRUE SECURITY IN PARADISE ESTATES!
The entire complex is surrounded by a moat in which crocodiles have been placed. Security guards patrol behind the barbed wire, and no one can enter or leave without your properly certified invitation.

Can it be that, as Harry Emerson Fosdick said in *God of Grace and God of Glory,* we are "rich in things and poor in soul"?

I don't mean millions, but whatever few dollars you and I have. What do our split-level fortresses, or even our two bedroom bungalows say to the people of the Third World? And how do they square with the wind-swept figure in the Palestinian night who had no place to lay his head? Was he an impractical dreamer, or did he know something? I am not a wealthy person, but compared to the disciples of Jesus I am a Croesus. I dine on the finest shining plates, with silver knives and spoons. I look out from air-conditioned comfort, through invisible walls. I bathe in shining porcelain, in delicious hot water. I open a door and find unspoiled food, which I pop into a miracle stove and cook in minutes. Can you see Simon Peter staring with astonishment at the wealth my simple home affords? How then will I respond to Jesus' words: "Go, sell what you have, and give to the poor, and you will have treasure in heaven; and come, follow me" (Mark 10:21). These are disturbing words. Must I take them literally? And if I take them even *seriously*, what will happen to my things?

II TOWARD A CHRISTIAN MATERIALISM

One who believes that God has become incarnate in Jesus Christ ought to look at that world in a different way. But how? In what sense is that way different from what we call (often negatively) *materialism*? I suppose nobody would come right out and claim to be a thoroughgoing materialist; most of us would say that some values have a higher importance than the world of things: love, friendship, etc. But some of us *live* as though there were nothing more important than the material world. Negatively, one can become an ascetic, and renounce the world of things in favor of sackcloth and ashes, or positively, one can seek to acquire as many things as possible. In either case, *things* become dominant. Sometimes, those who renounce the world spend more energy worrying about it (begging for meals, alms, shelter), while the wealthy take the world for granted and are, in a sense, less material-minded than their poorer cousins. But whichever way you approach it, you are a materialist if your life is governed by the physical world.

In what sense, then, is a Christian materialist different from a pure materialist? In this: the Christian is under orders to love the world, while the pure materialist is not! Sound strange? Yes, but the teachings of the Bible in general, and of Jesus in particular, lead to the conclusion

16

that those who follow Christ *ought* to love the world for which he died. His Cross not only set human souls right with God, but brought the whole created order back into right relationship with him, since, in our fall we seem to have brought the house down with us (Rom. 8:18-25). And thus we should love the world in a way in which I'm afraid most pure materialists do not.

Let me illustrate. Two men own sports cars. (If sports cars are not your "thing," you can substitute any material object for them in this story: house, jewelry, a stable of horses, a painting, or an old pair of shoes.) Now one of the men really loves his car. He takes care of it; he services it himself; he keeps it in perfect tune, and all shiny with wax and polish. When he drives it, he does so with great enjoyment and inner pleasure. As he negotiates a challenging corner, downshifting the synchromesh transmission, he is thinking, "What a beautiful car! What fun to drive, and how proud I am to take care of such a machine. I really love this car."

The other man owns an identical car. He too may take care of it as far as the spit and polish are concerned. But he doesn't really care too much whether it is in good tune, so long as it gives off a satisfactory roar and will outrun everything else on the road. When he drives it, he does so with great satisfaction because he feels that everyone is envious of him for owning so fine an automobile. He is thinking, "What a beautiful car. What fun it is to drive because it makes me feel like somebody special. I really love this car." But in fact he does not love the car at all. He loves himself, and the car is a means to self-gratification. The Christian, like God, ought to love the world (John 3:16).

17

Now of course we cannot love things in the same way that we love people. We can't even love pets in the same way; they haven't the capacity to respond. But this does not stop us from loving them. And we are indebted to the wise Jewish philosopher, Martin Buber, for introducing us to a new way of talking about such relationships. He wrote a marvelous little book called *I and Thou*. Unfortunately "thou" has somewhat lost its meaning for the average American. We usually think of it as formal, because we are accustomed to hear it as God is addressed in the Bible, or by people at public prayer. But in German (Buber's language), as in Spanish or French, "thou" is the *familiar,* not the formal usage. You would say "you" to a stranger, but "thou" to your fiancé. This distinction is still preserved among the old Friends' meetings in America, where the Quakers speak to one another with the loving use of the familiar "thee." So, in this book, if I talk about an *I-thou* relationship, I'm not speaking of a formal, stiff encounter between strangers, but a loving, intimate relationship between those who understand and appreciate each other.

Can you really have such a relationship with a thing? I believe so. If, when I look at a tree, I see only so many cords of stove wood, then the tree and I are in what Buber would call an *I-it* relationship. If I look at the ocean, and all I can think of is so many billion tons of cold salt water, then I'm having an *I-it* encounter with the sea. But if I can see that tree through the appreciative eyes of a retired forest ranger, or a landscape architect, or a traveler in need of shade—in other words, anybody who really cares about trees—then I may venture to call the tree *thou* rather than *it*. And if, like an

18

excited child, or a sailor with a faraway look in his eye, or any true lover of the never-ceasing surf, I can appreciate the ocean, then I can say *thou* to it. To truly love the world of things is to have a genuine relationship with them.

Even between persons an I-thou relationship is rare. It is a precious thing, like a good marriage, or an old friendship; a sudden glance of appreciation across a room, as if to say, "Yes, you and I understand each other, don't we?" If it is so hard to have such a relationship with people, how can we ever expect to do so with a thing? Well, in some ways it is easier, for things are more dependable. "Old dogs will love you, even when you're bad." And when you go home at night, no matter how poorly the world has treated you, the lamp, the easy chair, and the down comforter all say "Welcome home!" in their same old way.

You can probably tick off a long list of people who have had the I-thou relation with the world of things: John Muir, who said, "The mountains are calling, and I must go," and strode the Sierra Nevada in search of knowledge and beauty; St. Francis of Assisi, feeding the birds; Jesus or John the Baptist, seeking solace in the wilderness; Audubon, patiently painting America's birds.

Make your own list; include the woman down the street who tends her flower bed so lovingly, the mountain climbers who delight in "climbing clean," leaving neither scar nor piton to mark their passing, the young physician who spends time with his sons restoring a 1929 American la France fire truck, or the farmer who watches with deep satisfaction as the first spring plow turns the warm brown earth.

Can you put yourself on that list? How do you feel toward things? A Christian materialist is one who uses the world lovingly, appreciating things for their beauty or utility. He lives in harmony with the natural order, without upsetting the fragile balance of nature, by using the raw materials of the earth to build that which enobles and endures. Take a long hard look at the job at which you work, the place in which you live, and the things you do during your day.

> Do you keep your world neat?
> Are you thrifty?
> Do you have your car greased on schedule?
> When something breaks, do you fix it or throw it away?
> How often do you buy new clothes? Why?
> How fast do you eat?
> Do you ever take walks?
> How would you feel if your house burned down?
> Do you like the look and feel of fine leather or wood?

There are no right answers. These questions are not to test you, but to start you thinking about your attitude toward the material world. If you are alarmed by the way things seem to be going for Mother Earth, and if you are committed to Christ's lordship over you and the world, then you may want to make some changes in your life-style.

It's not just a matter of man against nature. We ourselves are part of the natural world, and when we are called upon to love and respect the world of material things, we also need to love and respect our own bodies.

They are, according to Paul, the temple of the Spirit (I Cor. 6:19-20). It is an act of worship (Rom. 12:1) to use them wisely and well. Our bodies, warts and all, are to be loved, not seen as traps in which we are confined. The old creation story makes it plain that the whole person (not just some invisible thing called the soul) is a thing of worth in God's eyes. It says, not that man was given a soul, but that man *became* a soul (Gen. 2:7). It says that, male and female, we are made in his image, and our sexuality is given his blessing (Gen. 1:28). And along with all the rest of creation, we are pronounced *good!* (Gen. 1:31).

We forget that we are part of nature. Just as a fish doesn't know that he is wet, and we don't think about the air we breathe until it somehow becomes scarce, we forget the natural element in which we daily live. We take our heartbeats and our brain waves for granted. When I "think," I do not think *about* electrical circuits operating in the brain, I think *by means of them,* and so I am unconscious of them. Indeed, I am likely to think of my thoughts as spiritual, or even holy, when they may be due simply to an upset stomach, or a very earthy desire. Certainly I want to transcend my flesh-and-blood nature, and even to discipline it to be obedient to my will. But I cannot escape being made of material things. That is why Paul cried, "Who will deliver me from this body of death?" (Rom. 7:24). But it is important to remember that the deliverer is Jesus Christ, who became flesh and blood, and who appreciated the material world as no other person. His birth in a manger in a sleepy Hebrew town is the entry of the holy into the unholy. It is the reversal of the Greek idea of the mortal flesh reaching up

toward the spiritual and unreachable. It is the eternal
coming into time and space and restoring it to its rightful
inheritance. You and I have no business looking at the
world through the eyes of critics; rather we are called
upon to love it, because God loved it, enough to send his
son into it and, at incredible cost, bring it home again.

That doesn't make the world perfect. We are still
plagued with inherited deformities, or tendencies to
disease. Those who say, "I find God in nature," had
better be pretty selective about what part of nature they
choose for a text. A hemophiliac child who has to be
stung by bees to speed up his clotting time, or a citizen of
Vestmannaeyjar, Iceland, whose home was wiped out by
a volcano in 1973, may have some reason for bitterness.
Landslides, tidal waves, floods, droughts, and tornadoes,
not to mention mosquitoes, staphylococcus bacteria, and
coral snakes make every natural theologian uneasy. But
they must be faced. Indeed part of what it means to have
an I-thou relationship with the world is to embrace its
pain as well as its pleasures. As I come to love in an old
friend many faults almost as though they were virtues, so
love for the world calls me to accept its incompleteness
(see Rom. 8:20-23).

Perhaps you can hear this better if I let you speak for a
moment to a friend of mine who was born without the
use of his legs. (I who have all my faculties, so far, have
not the right to say some of the things he can say.) He is
willing to talk very openly about his life as a cripple, and
he says something like this:

> I used to hate my body, and to hate God for giving it to me.
> But as I have grown older I have learned something about
> that anger. I still have it, but God has used it to give me wit,

22

skill, and strength of character that I would never have had if things had been easy for me. Out of the cross of my crippled legs has come a resurrection. I believe I am really somebody special, and I have learned to give thanks for what I am. When you leave this room, I may forget you, for you are an ordinary person, but you will never forget me—that fellow on crutches who told you that when God made you he did not make a mistake.

I don't know what I would be like, had I such odds to face, but I agree with him that the best way to handle the natural world, calamity and all, is to face it, not to pretend it away. When someone dies grief may be heavy upon us, but it is better to let ourselves grieve, to feel the anger and the estrangement, to cry and mourn, rather than pretend we are not deeply affected.

And that brings me to one final thing we must face about the world and ourselves if we are to have an I-thou relation. That is, like all friends, it was not meant to last forever. Let me confess to a private prejudice which I don't ask you to share. It is that I don't care for artificial flowers. Now that the art of making them out of plastic has been perfected, they can hardly be told from the real, and they are sometimes quite beautiful. But I have a sneaky feeling that flowers were not supposed to collect dust. They were made to bloom in fragile splendor for a time, and then be gone. If the forsythia, jonquils, and dogwood were blooming all the time we would probably quit noticing them. But when the hills are covered with the new miracle every spring, they become very precious indeed. I wonder if there isn't something a little immoral about making flowers that cannot die, a little like Adam and Eve's sin of wanting to be like God, who lives forever.

23

But never mind that. Whether my prejudice is true or not, it certainly is true that we shall all die. And that too is a fact of life that we must embrace and celebrate.

It is a sad fact that we humans, reluctant to admit the material nature of our existence, refuse to face facts about our declining bodies. Every day people die leaving no will, without making insurance plans, or discussing with their husbands and wives what burial plans would be meaningful to them both. "We were going to do that someday," they say. Our language is filled with euphemisms which cover up the fact of death: passed away, fell asleep, kicked the bucket. Morticians beautify corpses and make them look as if they were asleep, while flowers and soft music attempt to ease the blow and disguise the reality.

WOODSIDE MORTUARY
TAKES THE BOTHER OUT OF DYING

How much better than the grass and crepe paper disguising the earth would it be to show our grief by digging with real shovels into the burnt sienna of the soil, building a pine box, and letting our loved ones return to the dust from which they came. To embalm is to reach óut after immortality, to disguise the truth of our creaturehood, and in the long run to flee from loving the world in which we live.

To say *thou* to the word is to love it as God loves, while it is yet imperfect (Rom. 5:8; I John 4:10). It is to admire it as its Creator admired it when he called it good. It is to live in it in joyful partnership, as good stewards of our possessions. It is to grow old with gladness, knowing that

24

in our childhood we have one kind of kinship with the earth, and in old age, another. We may begin as inquisitive children, looking with wonder at spiders' webs, jet planes, earthworms, and stars, and end as older persons whose task it is to pass on that legacy of wonder to succeeding generations, spreading the joy of being human to those whom we bring into the world. Ideal humanity means sharing the world with others, even giving our eyes and our kidneys when we die to those who need them. It means making out our wills, being good stewards of the possessions we have accumulated over the years. It means seeing ourselves as part of the great dance, turning to the music of the spheres, in which all the stars of heaven and the atoms of the earth take part. It is a happy, good way to live. It knows pain, surely, but it takes even that into its bosom and bears it gladly, for to hurt is to be alive.

But that's enough poetry. Let's turn now to some hard facts, and let's begin with cold cash.

III MONEY

The organ plays while golden plates are passed among the people. Like the red felt in the plates, the music muffles the sound of clinking coins and the click of pocketbooks. At the ends of the pews, the ushers are standing in dignity, and we are all carefully not looking at one another as we send our treasure to the altar, for we know that alms should not be given before men. We each have our own thoughts.

Charles: *This was a hard-earned ten dollars. I sure hope it will be spent where it will do some good.*

Suzanne: *I'm glad I can give money. I'm so busy at the hospital I don't ever seem to have any time that I can give.*

Little Freddie *attending with his grandmother for the first time): I didn't know they were going to pass out money. I didn't take but a quarter.*

Arthur: *I've been giving fifty cents a week ever since I was a little kid.*

Ethel: *I'd feel better about giving if he wouldn't preach so much about politics.*

Esther: *I'd feel better about giving if he would preach more about what's going on in Washington.*

Richard (writing a check): I feel better knowing that this is deductible.

Pastor Smith: If only more of us were tithers, think what we could accomplish!

Little Phyllis: I wonder what Pastor Smith is going to do with all this money.

William (Chairman of the Board of Stewards): I hope we have a good day at the plate today.

Charlene (a widow): It's only a little—I wish it could be more.

Soon we have all contributed, and now the ushers march in solemn procession to the altar. The minister prays:

> O Lord, our God, send down upon us thy Holy Spirit, we beseech thee, to cleanse our hearts, to hallow our gifts, and to perfect the offering of ourselves to thee; through Jesus Christ our Lord.

Amen, say all the people, and he takes the plates, now filled with envelopes, checks, green paper, silver, and copper coins, and places them on the Lord's Table. A doxology is sung.

When you stop to think about it, this is a mysterious act. Is it a sacred or a secular business? What does it really mean? If an observer from another planet watched our activities without understanding the language, what do you think he would conclude? What would he make of the bits of paper and metal which we have carried to the high place of honor, and in the presence of which we have sung praises?

Coins, as we know them, were invented about seven hundred years before Christ by the Lydians, a people of

TRAVELING LIGHT

Asia Minor. (They also invented dice about the same time. Apparently gambling has a way of creeping in wherever money appears. I wonder who flipped the first coin to make a decision, and if it was heads or tails.) The Lydians must have made good use of their invention because Croesus (around 550 B.C.) became the richest monarch of his day, and his name has become a proverbial symbol for wealth, like that of Rockefeller or Getty in our day. The oldest paper money in existence is a Chinese bill of around A.D. 1300.

But we do not know who really invented the *idea* of money, for since the dawn of history men have used objects to represent value: bits of bronze, lumps of salt, clay tablets, or sea shells. The American Indians strung together beads made from sea shells into long, beautifully woven belts, called wampum. At first the value of coins was determined by their intrinsic worth: that is, coins were worth more or less according to their weight, purity, and the scarcity of the metal from which they were made. In other words, the more trouble it was to find a certain metal, the more it would be worth. Wampum took its value from the time and labor necessary to produce a string or belt of it. In other words, we might say money means trouble!

Money is a symbol: that is, it stands for something else. A word is a symbol. "Words" have no value of their own; they convey an idea or a meaning which may stand for something of value. However, words can come to be valued for their own sake; great poetry, prayers, passwords, or phrases such as "I love you," have power to move people. But of all the world's symbols, money is the one that most easily can become valued apart from the goods and services for which it stands. Sometimes misers refuse to put their money into banks because they like to count it, or look at it, or fondle it. But before you laugh too much at the miser, ask yourself how *you* feel when there is plenty of money in your purse or pocketbook. When you were a child, were you ever given a silver dollar by your favorite uncle? Or a package of absolutely brand-new unused pennies? What sort of feeling did you have about it?

Today, most countries issue token coins; that is, coins whose actual metal value is less than the money valuation stamped on them. That means that a nickel really isn't worth five cents. (You don't need to tell that to the average person! I heard of a man who went to buy washers recently, and found them selling for seven cents each. So he went home and bored holes in the middle of some nickels and used them!) Of course paper money has no intrinsic worth, it is supposed to represent gold or silver held in the vaults of the government that prints it, but you can no longer demand that the government give you the metal for which your dollar bill stands. There was a time when the United States had more than enough gold in its vaults to cover all the currency in circulation, but today the value of the dollar depends more on the strength and reputation of the country than on the price of gold.

Our economy has been in a gradual inflationary climb ever since the great depression of the thirties. This means that the purchasing power of the dollar becomes less and less. For instance, those who lived through World War II found that money which they had saved before the war was worth only about a third, in terms of what it would buy, in the 1950s. Those who are hurt most by inflation are persons whose income is fixed (such as someone who is living on the interest on savings) and the very poor. The poor suffer because nearly all of their income must be spent on food, rent, and other necessities, and rising costs hit them where it hurts. Only those who are fortunate enough to have some special items of luxury: coin collections, antiques, paintings, and the like, can turn inflation into a profit. For most of us, if our income doesn't keep pace with rising costs, things are tough.

The result of this continued inflation can produce some peculiar and tragic problems. A couple who were extremely modest in their needs, who had scrimped and saved according to all they had been taught about the value of frugality and common sense might find that their life savings are no longer capable of supporting them. (Indeed, Germany had such an inflation after World War I that people who had fixed incomes from bonds or insurance equal to five or six thousand dollars a year discovered that their whole year's income would not buy a loaf of bread!) We seem to have here some hard economic evidence that Jesus was right in telling the story about the talents (Matt. 25:14-30). A *talent* was originally a measure of weight, as many forms of money were (*cf.* the British "pound" for example). It was equivalent to about six-thousand *drachmas,* or pieces of silver. The RSV says that it was worth about a thousand dollars, but this is very misleading, because of the difference in purchasing power in biblical times. A drachma (Roman *denarius*) was a day's pay for a laborer (Matt. 20:2), which means that a talent could support a laboring man for more than sixteen years! In our day, the word talent has come full circle: instead of meaning money, it means the skills and abilities that can earn money!

You will remember that the third servant, who received the one talent, "went and dug in the ground and hid his master's money" (verse 18). The other two put their money to work and doubled it. In addition to the rich spiritual advice contained in the parable, apparently we have some good common sense about inflation: money was not meant to be hoarded; if you hoard it, you will lose it. This is the same advice, of course, that he gives to us about our spiritual values: "For whoever would save his life will lose it; and whoever loses his life for my sake, he will save it" (Luke 9:24). Some risk must be taken if we are to survive, either financially or morally.

As for what to do about inflation on the national or international level, you and I are about as good as the world's leading economists and financiers at discovering the solution. The head of the United States Cost of Living Council stated in 1974, "I don't believe it is clear that mankind today knows how to control inflation." Some of the "experts" think that governments should cease to concern themselves about inflation and deflation, letting nature take its course. Others think that governments should actively try to keep the economy on an even keel, discouraging booms by such means as cutting down on public works or raising interest rates, or, in the case of deflation, by launching great building programs and lowering rates of interest. But whatever they do, somebody gets caught. If inflation is cut back through government controls, then unemployment in-

31

creases. Those who keep their jobs like for the government to intervene, while those who are laid off are not so certain. Apparently *some* government intervention is necessary, but just how much?

As for those of us middle-income families caught in the squeeze between prices that are rising rapidly and income that is lagging behind, there are some ways of economizing. The most common place where inflation hurts, and where we can really do something about it, is the food budget. By growing our own vegetables and by judicious shopping (avoiding instant foods, buying in bulk, using the super market's own cheaper brands), as much as a thousand dollars a year can be trimmed off a family budget. It also helps to make your own clothing, to use public transportation where possible, and to conserve energy by weather stripping and insulating. During inflationary times we ought to be careful particularly about borrowing money or running up finance charges on credit cards. You might even consider riding a bicycle to work! But suppose you are doing all these things and the squeeze is still tight. How can you avoid worrying yourself to death over money? Let's face it—it's tough to be an ordinary citizen in these days. Most of us are preoccupied with making ends meet. Can you do this, and still have a Christ-like attitude toward the material world?

One way that will help is to make sure that we are seeing money as a *means* and not as an *end*. When money becomes an end, that is when we desire it for its own sake, we tend to think about it more and more, and to forget the true happiness that ought to be the desired end. For example:

Sandy's neighbor, Charley, owns a self-contained recreational vehicle, for which he paid eight thousand dollars. He
and his family travel all over the U.S. on their vacation,
carrying their motel with them. They have a marvelous
vacation every year. Sandy is jealous of Charley. "If only I
had eight thousand dollars," he thinks, "we could see the
country, too." But he doesn't need eight thousand dollars to
see the country. He could do it for five hundred with an old
station wagon, a secondhand tent, and a Coleman stove.
Judicious planning, reservations at camping areas, and
family cooperation could make for an exciting outing. In fact,
Sandy's family might come back better refreshed, more
satisfied, and with their family life strengthened. The *end* is
not the money, or the self-contained camper, but a happy
family outing. And that can be had practically for free.

Jesus knew that money is a means and not an end. When
he said to his disciples, "Do not lay up for yourselves
treasures on earth, where moth and rust consume and
where thieves break in and steal, but lay up for
yourselves treasures in heaven." (Matt. 6:19-20), he was
warning them not to confuse temporary earthly values
with permanent spiritual values. The things of earth are
good (see Gen. 1:31), but they are not *gods*. Remember
that the word *God* and the word *good* come from the
same root. Consider "good-bye," the meaning of which is
God be with you, or "gospel," the meaning of which is
God's spiel or good news.

When we seek our happiness in anything less than
God, we are doomed to failure. And when we use a mere
symbol, like money, as an end in itself, we are in trouble.
Of course, this is nothing new. Lucretius wrote in *On
The Nature of Things:* "Afterwards wealth was discovered and gold found out, which soon robbed of their
honors the strong and beautiful alike, for men, however

33

valiant and beautiful of person, generally follow in the train of the richer man. But were a man to order his life by the rules of true reason, a frugal subsistence joined to a contented mind is for him great riches" (book V, p. 1105). Or John Stuart Mill, in *Utilitarianism,* who wrote what a bad thing it was that "what was once desired as an instrument for the attainment of happiness, has come to be desired for its own sake" (chapter 4). Or the writer of the Nineteenth Psalm: "the ordinances of the Lord are true, and righteous altogether. More to be desired are they than gold" (verses 9-10). But it is a lesson we have never completely learned, and so we must listen to the nagging voice again.

Besides, we are guilty of going a step further. Not only have we confused means with ends, but even when we have understood that money is only a means, we have chosen the wrong *ends.* This was said in its most classical form by the American economist, Thorstein Veblin, in a book called *The Theory of the Leisure Class,* 1899. He coined the phrase "conspicuous comsumption" to describe the way in which we spend our money, not to meet our needs for food, shelter, and clothing, but to impress our neighbors. More recently, the books of Vance Packard, such as *The Status Seekers,* have carried the same theme. In common American parlance, this is known as keeping up with the Joneses. We use our money to impress others with our worth. Here are some ways to get "one up" on your neighbors.

> When you buy a new color television, be sure to leave the box that it came in lying out in the yard for several days so they will all know you own one. (If you can't afford to buy the television, just pick up the box behind the appliance store on

the trash bin and leave *it* in your yard for a while.) It is worth noting that when electricity first came to rural America, it was customary to put the washing machine or the refrigerator *on the front porch,* so the neighbors would know that you had one.

Decorate your home from the outside in. Never mind what the inside walls are like; make sure the part that people see is trimmed, clipped, and painted. Live as though the house were for them, and not for you and your children.

Buy a yellow sports car.

There are plenty of others, just as ridiculous. If you can't afford to follow this route, you might try the method known as reverse snobbery, in which you wear shabby clothes and drive your car till the wheels fall off, just to prove that you are so far above money worries you don't have to look fancy.

But if you think those suggestions are absurd, face in all honesty the question: Why *did* you buy the house you are living in? The car you drive? The clothes you wear? Why did you pick that particular style? How often do you trade cars? If you buy a new one every year you are losing thousands of dollars in depreciation. Why not put 150,000 miles on it before you trade it? So long as it is still getting you there, what difference does it make if the inside is a little dingy and the rust is beginning to form around the edges? Could it be that status is the sneaky reason?

Once a very wealthy young man came to Jesus, seeking the clue to happiness. He got started on the wrong foot by calling Jesus "good," to which the Lord replied, "Why do you call me good? No one is good but God alone" (Mark 10:18. There are those two words again—this time they're equated: God = good). This means that we must be very careful what we worship. Not even the wisest teacher, or the greatest king, can be called God. Then Jesus told him to keep the commandments. But notice an interesting thing: Jesus listed only part of the ten laws. The ones he listed (Mark 10:19) are the ones he knew the young man had kept since childhood. The others he knew the young man had not kept. They are the last one, "You shall not covet," and the first four, all of which have to do with worshiping God. In other words, Jesus knew that the young man had made a god out of his money. That is what is keeping him from happiness. So Jesus offered him the only road to happiness that the young man could follow. It is a tough, terrible law. "Go," he said, "sell what you have, and give to the poor, and you will have treasure in heaven; and come, follow me" (verse 21)." But the young man could not give up his god, so he went away depressed.

Does this mean that we must all sell everything and become street preachers like Jesus? That depends. It depends on what or who your god is. If, like this young man, you are worshiping *things,* then yes, you do need to follow that law to find happiness. If you worship God, and can use money as a means to serve him in gladness, then you may keep your house and your boat for awhile yet. But note two things:

1) We are all in some ways like that young man, and will never get to heaven (not until a camel goes through a needle's eye—verse 25) unless the miracle of God's grace makes it possible (verse 27), and,

2) Sooner or later you will have to give it all up, every bit of it. You can't take it with you.

IV SUBDUING THE EARTH

"You can't take it with you." Yes, but in the meantime, what do you do with it? How do we manage the material world so that we use it, rather than it using us? How do we keep it as a means, rather than an end? We have had our marching orders from the beginning. According to Genesis, God's first words to his newly created couple have to do with responsibility for the world of things: "Be fruitful and multiply, and fill the earth and subdue it; and have dominion over the fish of the sea and over the birds of the air and over every living thing that moves upon the earth" (1:28).

As far as the first half of that commandment is concerned, most moderns will agree that we have done a pretty good job of obeying it. We have certainly multiplied! We have not only filled the earth, we are about to overflow it. Depending on what doomsday prophet you read, there will be standing room only within thirty to three hundred years. Then what? But even before then, what does it mean to subdue the earth?

Except for nest-building birds, beavers, and a few insects, nearly all wild creatures are content to use the universe just as they find it. The cattle stand in the fields "blown by all the winds that pass and wet with all the showers." Bears, like our primitive ancestors, sleep in natural caves or hollow logs. Migrating plains animals move as they are forced by the changing seasons to find forage. Birds fly south for the winter. It is nature that determines what they do.

But men and women do battle with the elements. We refuse to be driven before the coming winter. Instead, we make fires, build warm shelters, skin animals for their fur. We store food and learn how to preserve it, to see us through the long winter night. It seems like a long jump from the first crude campfire to modern central heating, or from salting venison to the automatic, self-defrosting electric refrigerator, but the principle is the same. There is a bigger jump between beast and primitive man than there is between *Pithecanthropos erectus* and his twentieth-century descendants. Whatever else it means to be created in the image of God, it certainly means that we are to be shapers of the world. But what form shall this shaping take? Do we try to interfere with nature as little as possible, or do we devote ourselves constantly to changing the face of the planet? There is a theory that sabbath-keeping among the early Hebrews began as a weekly reminder that we, too, are a part of the created order, and that at least one day out of seven we must recognize the right of all things to be undisturbed by man; hence no plowing on the sabbath, not even the removal of a stone from its rightful resting place.

The tipi is much better to live in; always clean, warm in winter, cool in summer; easy to move. The white man builds big house, cost much money, like big cage, shut out sun, can never move; always sick. Indians and animals know better how to live than white man; nobody can be in good health if he does not have all time fresh air, sunshine and good water. If the Great Spirit wanted men to stay in one place he would make the world stand still; but He made it to always change, so birds and animals can move and always have green grass and ripe berries, sunlight to work and play, and night to sleep; summer for flowers to bloom, and winter for them to sleep; always changing; everything for good; nothing for nothing.

The white man does not obey the Great Spirit; that is why the Indians could never agree with him.[1]

By the time we get to the fourth chapter of Genesis, we see our first evidence that the Hebrew people were divided on the matter. Some of them (the spiritual descendants of Cain) were agrarian people, who lived in towns, cultivated fields, and built houses for themselves. Others (followers of Abel) were nomads, keeping flocks and wandering from oasis to oasis, wherever nature would supply water. This distinction between the settler and the wanderer has continued down to our own day. These two points of view can be neatly seen in the persons who went west during the 1800s in America. There were the settlers and the pioneers. The settlers built fences and the cowboys cut them down. One group wanted security and the other wanted freedom. The farmers wanted rules; the cattlemen wanted adventure. If the first fight in human history was between a farmer and a herdsman (Gen. 4:1-16), then the American west continued the battle. Remember the plot of *Oklahoma!* summarized by the song that said, "the farmer and the cowman should be friends!"

For the Hebrews, the sentiment was usually on the side of the wanderer, not the city-dweller. (Abel is the

[1] M. I. McCreight, *Firewater and Forked Tongues* (Pasadena, Calif.: Trail's End Publishing Co., 1947), p. 61. Quoting Chief Flying Hawk, a Sioux Indian.

sympathetic character in the story of the first murder).
Even after the desert wanderings and settling down in
the permanent cities of the land of Caanan, the Hebrews
venerated their tent-dwelling ancestors. Regularly they
celebrated the feast of booths (Lev. 23:33-43, Neh.
8:13-18; John 7:2) to remind themselves of their origins
as a desert people with no permanent home. They held
their ascetic brothers, the Rechabites (Jer. 35), in high
esteem because they were "tent-dwellers." Even the
word for God's dwelling with men (John 1:14, Rev. 21:3)
comes from the verb meaning "to pitch a tent." As the old
Hebrew "tent of meeting" symbolized God in the midst,
so in the person of Jesus is God "camping out" with his
nomad children in a hostile world. It is not surprising,
then, that Jesus should come as one who thought little of
such things as food and shelter. He was content to pick
up a little food in the grain fields and to depend on his
heavenly Father to feed him, as he feeds the birds of the
air and the lilies of the field.

But how are his followers to live? If we thought (as
some of the New Testament writers evidently did—see
Luke 9:27, I Thess. 4:13-18, Rev. 22:20) that the end of
the world were going to take place very shortly, perhaps
we could give a relatively simple answer. And, indeed,
whenever there have been movements that prophesied
the imminent return of Christ there have been people
who got rid of their earthly possessions, even to the point
of committing economic suicide, in anticipation of the
new age. Furthermore, there is good reason to look at life
with this sort of "living on borrowed time" attitude. For
one thing, the end of the world will come for everyone
who reads these words before another hundred years

have passed; none of us will be here after that. Moreover, even though modern science has delivered us from the diseases that struck down our grandparents when they were young (pneumonia, scarlet fever, etc.), there is no assurance that an accident, a rare virus, or a simple heart attack might get us at any moment. We had better live as those who are about to die!

The New Testament church, probably partly because of their feeling that Christ was going to return very soon and partly because of their new sense of being liberated in Christ, experimented for a time with a form of communal living. "And all who believed were together and had all things in common; and they sold their possessions and goods and distributed them to all, as any had need" (Acts 2:44-45). This was apparently not a systematic or carefully thought out form of government, such as a highly-organized political state would be. They were constantly revising it as needs arose (see Acts 6:1-7), and it did not last as an institution within the church. It was a natural result of a new-found spirit of generosity and hope among the newly baptized, and an obedient response to the teachings of Jesus that we should minister to each other's material needs (Matt. 25:34-35; John 21:17).

Although the pure sharing community of the church described in Acts 2 may be rare among middle-class Christians today, we still find, in every healthy congregation, results of the same Christ-inspired mutual concern. Particularly is this true when a crisis occurs, such as a death or a home destroyed by fire. We are almost too eager to fill the bereaved house with casseroles or to collect second-hand furniture and clothing for our dislocated neighbors. Almost every church has a fund for the care of the poor and needy, and a portion of the annual budget is earmarked for them. But we live in a very different world from that of Acts 2. Those first Christians came from among the lower economic classes, and they badly needed one another, not only for sharing food and funds, but also for mutual protection from their enemies (see Acts 8:1). As long as the church is a persecuted minority, it has no trouble forming communities of concern. But when the Emperor Constantine (or the President) is a Christian, and our religion is socially acceptable, then we have a hard time knowing how to unite in our charitable works.

How does the church relate to the world? Are we the world's enemy or its friend? Throughout our history there has been a battle between these two views, like the fight between cowboys and farmers, which started with Abel and Cain. That portion of Christendom which would withdraw from the world and have little security in it we can call the *sect*. Those who would work comfortably alongside the world we can call the *church*. Generally we think of the sects as groups like those Protestant denominations which broke away from organized Christianity to form "unworldly" communities, like the Quakers or the New England Puritans. It is characteristic of the sect that it is concerned with personal piety and salvation and stays out of politics and social action, except as these speak to the conditions of its own members.

But every sect discovers at once that it has to use "worldly" methods of organizing, raising funds, building places of worship, and teaching its young, or else it will die out in a generation. (This in fact has happened to many of them, notably the Shaker community which separates their men and women and so produces few future Shakers!) And things almost never turn out to be quite as idyllic and pure as the founders hope. Listen to the disappointed words of Governor William Bradford, writing about the colony at New Plymouth:

> The failure of this experiment of communal living, which was tried for several years, and by good and honest men, proves the emptiness of the theory of Plato and other ancients, applauded by some of later times—that the taking away of private property, and the possession of it in community, by a commonwealth, would make a state happy and flourishing; as if they were wiser than God. For in this instance, community of property (so far as it went) was found to breed much confusion and discontent, and retard much employment which would have been to the general benefit and comfort. . . . As for men's wives who were obliged to do service for other men, such as cooking, washing their clothes, etc., they considered it a kind of slavery, and many husbands would not brook it. This feature of it would have been worse still if they had been of an inferior class.[2]

Moreover, the moral life of the community, perhaps as a kind of rebellion against its strict Puritan rules, was outrageous! Apparently you cannot quite get away from the world by forming a sect, even if you move your base of operations to a new continent.

By the same token, no "church" can exist without elements of pietism within it. If the church becomes completely wedded to secular ways, it loses its soul, which is what happened to medieval Christianity and

[2] William Bradford, *The History of Plymouth Colony,* Harold Paget, ed., Classics Club College Ed. (New York: MacMillan, 1948), p. 151.

made the Reformation necessary. But within the medieval church, it was sect-like groups, such as the monastic orders, who kept the faith alive. It was monks, withdrawing from the world, who kept busy copying the Scriptures and thus enabled the data of the faith to survive during the Dark Ages. It was similar orders that kept alive the missionary movement or the arts of healing. It is almost as though the church, or those within it, have to withdraw from the world in order to see it objectively, but must return to the world in order to serve it as Christ would have us serve it.

In many ways, we would all like to be able to "get away from it all," and live on a tropical island as in *Swiss Family Robinson* or *Robinson Crusoe*. But note that neither of these celebrated adventures in private community would have been possible had it not been for the rest of the world. Mr. Robinson and his children made trip after trip to the wreck of their ship, which had been outfitted for the settling of a new colony (and had on it a rich variety of stores), and lived their exile in relative comfort with everything from cows to a candelabra. And Robinson Crusoe made twelve such trips, and said of the last:

> I discovered a locker with drawers in it, in one of which I found two or three razors and one pair of large scissors, with some ten or a dozen of good knives and forks; in another I found about thirty-six pounds value in money, some European coin, some Brazil, some pieces of eight, some gold, some silver.
>
> I smiled to myself at the sight of this money. "O drug!" said I aloud, "what art thou good for? Thou art not worth to me, no, not the taking off of the ground; one of those knives is worth all this heap; I have no manner of use for thee; e'en

remain where thou art and go to the bottom as a creature whose life is not worth saving." However, upon second thoughts, I took it away.[3]

There is an old saying: "One can get alone very well without a watch . . . provided everybody else owns one." So the desert island community can be fun, provided it is well stocked with the supplies of a technically competent civilization. We can't withdraw from the world altogether! No matter how choked it may be with selfishness and greed, we feed upon it. Pure as the church would be, its buildings are built on ground purchased from secular realtors with secular dollars. It names colleges after tobacco merchants who leave millions in their estates. I may arise this day, intending to be free from all materialist thoughts—a spiritual being. But even if I flee my air-conditioned bedroom to a cave, I will still be sitting on very material ground. Only in heaven are physical facilities unnecessary (Rev. 21:22).

Well, if I can't escape the material world, can I not at least keep it simple? "Yes," answered Henry David Thoreau. Referring to his own famous experiment in living off the land at Walden Pond, he wrote: "I find by my own experience, a few implements, a knife, an ax, a spade, a wheelbarrow, etc., and for the studious, lamplight, stationary, and access to a few books, rank next to necessaries, and can all be obtained at a trifling cost."[4]

[3] Daniel Defoe, *Robinson Crusoe* (New York: Walter J. Black, 1941), pp. 55-56.
[4] Henry David Thoreau, *Walden* (Roslyn, N.Y.: Walter J. Black, Inc., 1942), p. 358.

But for all his "rugged individualism" and independence, Thoreau was not much of an outdoorsman in the true sense. He certainly did not have the survival techniques or the knowledge of a Euell Gibbons, and he lived on a piece of land which belonged to somebody else. I have even heard it suggested that he borrowed the ax mentioned above. At any rate, James Russell Lowell says of him: "Mr. Thoreau seems to me to insist in public on going back to flint and steel, when there is a matchbox in his pocket which he knows very well how to use at a pinch."[5]

Again: It is possible to lead a simple, trouble-free life, if somebody else will let me use his yard to camp in and borrow his phone if I need an appendectomy.

But suppose we should all agree to get together and plan an ideal community. Since the beginning of history, in tribe, community, family, and nation, men and women have been trying to do this after a fashion. In our day we have been conscious of many groups living in communes, attempting to rediscover "mother earth," with great emphasis on organic gardening, pollution-free methods of heating, and a kind of free life-style for their members. But this is not a new idea. It has been the practice for untold centuries in African villages. And in America, ever since the discovery of this land by the white man, we have been displacing Indian communes and experimenting with our own. In the early 1800s there were over a hundred experimental communities established in America, the most famous of which were Robert Owen's experiment called New Harmony in

[5] Jerry Richard, ed., *The Good Life* (New York: Mentor Books, 1973), p. 87. From an essay on Thoreau.

46

Indiana and the Oneida Community in central New York. Although none of them were what we would call successful, some lasted for several years and left us a legacy of what not to do to achieve the good life. In our time, the most famous community is not a real one but a fictional one, called Walden II in a book by B. F. Skinner. His philosophy of behaviorism claims that we can teach people to learn to work together efficiently by offering the right incentives to them.

Perhaps the most ambitious attempt the world has ever seen at a community life-style, is the global movement called *communism*. Unfortunately, what success it has had has been at the expense of individual freedom, and often under totalitarian dictatorships who maintained their power with the use of concentration camps and systematic "disposal" of any opposition. As these words are being written, Alexander Solzhenitsyn is releasing for publication the second volume of his trilogy, *The Gulag Archipelago,* which tells the frightening story of the forced-labor system under Lenin and Stalin. Perhaps it is possible to bring off a successful communistic society without resorting to totalitarian means, but it would require an almost fanatical devotion to the cause on the part of all participants and a willingness to give up individual rights for the greatest good of the greatest number. From what we know of human nature, a society of such persons would be hard to find.

In capitalistic countries, the principal of selfishness is used as the fundamental incentive to keep the economy healthy. It is maintained that, free enterprise built upon competition and advertising keep the money and services flowing. The theory of production developed by

Adam Smith in his book called *The Wealth of Nations* became the philosophy of the new nation's economics, just as Jefferson's ideals became its political philosophy. It was Smith who coined the phrase "division of labor," which made possible the modern assembly line for more efficient production. Most Americans will agree that our *laissez-faire* economy has made a good life for us but it is by no means perfect. As we shall see in the next chapter, there is much suffering on the part of the very poor, and even the well-to-do are beginning to feel the pinch of runaway inflation. There is a modern-day version of the Rip Van Winkle story that goes something like this:

> A man was put to sleep for seventy-five years in a state of suspended animation. When he awoke, the first thing he wanted to know was what had happened to his stocks, which in 1974 had had a value of $25,000. So he picked up a phone and called his old brokerage office. When they finally found his records, he was informed that the market value of his portfolio was now more than thirty million dollars. But as he danced with elation, he was interrupted by a recording on the telephone which said: "Deposit $125 for the next three minutes."

This frightening story is not as far-fetched as we might think, for seventy-five years of 10 percent inflation would just about produce that situation.

The truth is that the world in which we, as twentieth-century men and women, find ourselves is really one large commune. Jet travel and television have reduced the barriers of space between us, and our economic interdependence has become a reality. We may not be members of the Common Market, but what happens to the economy of Europe or Asia has a great effect on us. If we have not been able to manage the mess that we have in small communes like New Harmony, will we ever be able to do it on a global scale? It is a question that we had better trouble ourselves with, not only because we are under divine orders to subdue the earth, but also because ominous clouds are on the horizon, warning us that if we do not achieve a solution in the very near future, the resulting chaos may lead to starvation for the peoples of the underdeveloped nations and perhaps even war and nuclear destruction for the more wealthy ones. Jesus promised us (Matt. 6:33) that if we would seek first his Father's kingdom, that "all these things" would be ours in addition. His words give us hope for a coming time of plenty when, "the plowman shall overtake the reaper and the treader of grapes him who sows the seed; and the mountains shall drip sweet wine" (Amos 9:13).

There *is* a solution to the problem of things and their tyranny. But we have to look squarely at the facts, no matter how harsh they are. How do we seek the kingdom of God from a world in danger of starving to death? We need to take an honest look at that world before we begin to formulate an answer. So then, let's face the grimmest specter of all, described in Rev. 6:5-6 as a rider on a black horse. His name is Famine.

V HUNGER

There is no more dreadful word in the English language. People die from thirst or from suffocation or from disease, but such deaths are relatively quick. Hunger can take a lifetime to kill, leaving in its wake a terrible collection of side effects: mental retardation, loss of dignity, slavery, and despair. It can even happen without people ever knowing it! In villages in Africa and South America, people are feasting happily on the manioc plant, making a kind of spoonbread from the root, and cooking the greens like collards or spinach. But there is little or no protein in their diet, and they grow up unknowingly starving their bodies and, what is worse, their brains. And this is happening not only in the underdeveloped countries, but within the shadows of American church steeples, not far from our affluent suburbs.

In 1973 at the University of Georgia, several hundred Christians from the Third World, in government, industry, medicine, banking, and the church, all gathered with the common purpose of struggling with the hunger problem. While they were there, the committee in charge of the worship pulled a trick on them. At one of the meals, waiters in the restaurant were instructed to serve a full meal only to every *third* person. The next person received a bowl of rice; and the next,

50

nothing at all. Normal table talk and manners continued for a while. Many of those with plenty *failed to notice* that those to their left and right had little or nothing. Instead, they went right on eating and chatting. Meanwhile, those not served felt a mounting anger. For a time it seemed that fights might even break out. Then, gradually, it began to dawn on the whole assembly that unless they began to share, some people were going to go hungry. Then a lot of happy things began to happen. People used their saucers and salad plates to spoon helpings of rice for their neighbors. Meat and vegetables, silverware and plates were shared. Good humor and even joy came over the group. And when the clean-up committee came, they found the table littered with leftovers, even though only one-third of the standard fare had been served (see Mark 6:43)!

Why not the world? For that banquet was a microcosm of the human race, of which, we are told: one-third have plenty to eat; one-third have a bare subsistence; one-third are starving. (That may be optimistic. Robert S. McNamara, president of the World Bank, in an address to the University of Notre Dame said, "One-half of humanity is hungering at this very moment."[1]) According to Church World Service, fifteen-thousand persons per day are dying of starvation, and five-thousand of them are women and children. It is hard for us to realize, since we live in a land of plenty, with teeming supermarket shelves, but even in America there are millions who do not have enough to eat. In 1967, a

---

[1] Quoted in *Sometimes They Cry*, H. F. Halverstadt and Estelle Rountree, ed. (New York: Friendship Press, 1970), p. 27.

survey of nine-hundred low-income rural homes in a southern state found that: 71 percent of the families had meat twice or less during the week, and 23 percent had *no* meat. Eighty percent had fresh fruit twice or less during the week, and 44 percent had *no* fresh fruit. Fifty-five percent had fresh milk twice or less, and 30 percent had *no* fresh milk.

At hearings in that state the following year, Dr. Alan Mermann, professor of pediatrics at Yale, told the U. S. Commission on civil rights that some 80 percent of the children he examined had "anemia sufficient to require treatment in any doctor's office anywhere in the country." He concluded:

> There is another area which . . . I think is very, very critical. . . . If the parent cannot feed his child, or her child, as parents feel a child should be fed, this produces a certain apathy and perhaps a mistrust . . . of the adult world when those earliest crying infant needs are not being met properly. This I think has profound influence on the way one sees the world from then on.[2]

What *would* it be like not to have enough to eat, for you and your children? How would you maintain your dignity, or keep from stealing? The question goes deeper than survival. It is possible on the most desperate terms, even in concentration camps and on life boats. But could you live with joy and dignity under such conditions? In 1970, a typical welfare budget allowed approximately nineteen cents per person per meal. Could you shop on that budget? Have you priced beans and potatoes lately? The following menu is described as normal for welfare families:

[2]*Ibid.,* p. 65.

Breakfast	1 glass of water or cup of coffee
	1 slice of toast with margarine
Lunch	1 peanut butter and jelly sandwich
	1 glass of Kool-Aid
Dinner	macaroni and cheese
	(or cabbage and neck bones)
	(or collards and rice)
	1 cup of tea

What did *you* have for dinner yesterday?

Worse still, even if we could suddenly feed everybody, how do we stop the increase in people? Listen once again to the frightening news:

Date		Estimated World Population
1	Time of Christ	250 million
1500	Reformation (Columbus)	500 million
1800	Napoleon	1,000 million
1914	World War I	2,000 million
Today		4,000 million

Note that it doubled in fifteen centuries, then again in three centuries, then in one, then in less than one. If the present rate continues, it will be eight billion in thirty years.[3] (If your fountain-pen cap were enlarged a billion times, it could contain the earth.) Will you be able to sit down in the year 2000?

Meanwhile, the land is not increasing. Tragically, most of this growth is taking place in those sections of the world where the land is undeveloped and hunger already

[3]*Ibid.*, p. 21.

is rampant. It has been estimated that about four-fifths of the new population will be in such areas. In countries like America, the growth has begun to reach zero. While in Asia and Africa many struggle to survive on less than one hundred dollars a year, the affluent 20 percent use 80 percent of the world's goods.

We need not take comfort in the fact that we live in a land of plenty. Someone has suggested that for Americans to call attention to starvation in the underdeveloped nations is somewhat like a man in one end of a life boat saying to another, "Friend, your end of the boat is sinking." We are in this boat together. Moreover, we who are affluent are contributing to the problem. We are increasingly becoming meat-eaters and this is the least efficient use of food. We have doubled our intake of beef per capita, yet cattle use up *seven* times the amount of grain that bread uses to produce the same amount of protein. Dr. James Cogswell, director of the Hunger Task Force for the Presbyterian Church, U.S., says that the amount of fertilizer used on our lawns, golf courses, and graveyards would satisfy India's agricultural needs.

There is talk these days of building the United States into a self-contained economic power which will have no need of trade with the rest of the world for food or energy. But when the rich man in Jesus' parable began to be thus satisfied, God called him a fool and took his life (Luke 12:16-21). In another story, Jesus describes a rich man as experiencing hell through his failure to feed the hungry beggar at his doorstep (Luke 16:19-31). No other command of Jesus is more clear than his order to feed the hungry. For those who do not, he gives orders that they be cast out into punishment (see Matt. 25:31-46). It is not that God arbitrarily punishes the wealthy and rewards the poor—it is that riches themselves carry the seeds of destruction in them (see Matt. 19:23-24). Our relative wealth compared to the rest of the world may lead us to become more and more defensive and possessive. The most ominous predictions picture America and Europe as armed camps under siege by the billions from the starving continents, defending ourselves against the ragged armies with the horror of nuclear weapons. At best, almost, we have a vision of watching television while our neighbors die.

But it does not have to end that way. As an evangelist might shout in a sawdust tent at the end of the service to the unconverted in his audience, "There is still time, brother!" But the time is desperately short. And the means at our disposal are few. What can we do, as a church, and as individual Christians who care? World hunger is a world problem and of course we cannot solve it alone, but we can begin with ourselves, our attitudes, and our strength. Feeble as one individual or church may be, if we begin to act, and others begin to act with us, we will be stronger than we think.

1. Right at the first, we can pray. Sometimes prayer is placed at the end of a list of things to do in an emergency, as though it were a last resort, or a final catchall, but it ought to be first. It is not as though God needed to know of the needs of the hungry earth—he knows our needs even before we ask him. But we do have from him a promise, not of stones, but of bread (Matt. 7:7-11), and when we begin to establish daily habits of prayer, they begin to affect our attitude and our life-styles. Probably, if all the Christians of the world were *praying* regularly

about world hunger, we would find our *living* altered to reflect the simplicity of Christ and the care which his followers owe to the poor.

2. We can make conscious effort to live as good stewards of the earth and its food. Even simple rules like not running the dishwasher unless it is full or saving aluminum cans for recycling, can begin to make a difference in the world's energy. Beyond that, we can learn to eat only what we need and to preserve leftovers. Many of us eat far too much and would be in much better health if we cut back. In a world where from 20 to 50 percent of us are going hungry, can we in good conscience allow ourselves to be overindulgent?

3. We can establish patterns of generosity for our personal lives that will eventually spill over into our giving as a church or as a nation. What would happen if each of us would set a minimum limit of 2 percent of our annual income to be set aside to give to development causes: Church World Service; the United Nations, the Food and Agricultural Organization, or the World Health Organization. We have not stretched our generosity nearly as far as it can go. Perhaps with our few loaves and fish a multitude could be fed!

4. We can become informed about every aspect of the problem. We need to keep well informed about legislation that is pending in Congress to help the situation, so that we can write to our representatives of our support. But we also need to be informed in a different way: we need to know with sensitivity what the deep feelings are of a person who is hungry. Of course we cannot expect to put ourselves exactly in the shoes of starving people, but as we get the facts about welfare meals and subsistence

diets we can be helped to be better stewards of what we have and use our resources with generosity to reach out to others.

5. We can begin to take a courageous stand to persuade our leaders and through them those of other countries that the time has come for basic and radical action. Recently (May 22, 1974), a resolution was introduced in the United States Senate (resolution no. 329) by Hubert Humphrey and two other senators urging that:

—the U.S. contribution "to the growing economic and human crisis in the developing world" be primarily in the form of food and the means and technology to produce it;

—food aid be expanded through Public Law 480, the Food for Peace Program, which has been seriously curtailed since 1972;

—the U.S. increase its matching pledge to the World Food Program for 1975-76 and encourage other nations to do likewise;

—the President and the secretary of state seek the participation of other major food exporting nations in this emergency effort, proportionate to their share of world food exports, and encourage oil producing nations to contribute a fair share;

—the U.S. announce its desire to work with the oil exporting and other nations in a major effort to increase world fertilizer production;

—the President encourage the American people to reduce the non-critical, non-food producing uses of fertilizer to make available increased supplies for food production purposes in the United States and elsewhere.

In introducing this resolution, Senator Humphrey stated: "The requirements of this grave hour must be met and not left to chance. Delay means lives. Delay also means less time for a well-planned response. Now is the time to respond to this emergency." Our legislators need to know that they have the full support of concerned Christian people as they seek to enable our nation to fulfill its role in the face of increasing hunger among the poor nations of the world.

But do we not need to go even further than that? How much money does our nation spend on space exploration? How much on defense? It has been estimated that one-fifth of our annual defense budget would fund a mass education effort for the world on birth control. Others have suggested that the money we spent getting to the moon could have enabled the food production rate of the world to catch up with population growth, if it had been spent on fertilizer instead. Of that, none of us can be sure, but we can be sure that we are in a radically dangerous situation, and that some kind of radical surgery is necessary. If not here, where should it be?

One final word on hunger: the voice of many critics of our nation's programs of welfare and foreign aid can be heard on every hand, making noises like this: "What good will it do to pour good money down that drain?" "The deadbeats of the world are just waiting for us to give them a handout, and they are snickering at us behind our backs." "Why give money to those who aren't willing to work for it?" Of course there *are* deadbeats on the welfare roles, and among the hungry peoples of the world. There have always been lazy beggars in human society. But the plain facts of the case are these: *most of the poor people of the world would be happy to work and do their share if only they could.* A welfare worker of my acquaintance says that for every freeloader she has met, she knows a hundred poor persons who have a fierce and independent pride. She names one family that refuses to accept welfare aid and exists on fried potatoes and grits rather than "live off our neighbors." The truth is that grinding poverty grinds people down. They cannot lift themselves up by their bootstraps. Our present international structure of economic relationships impoverishes the developing nations, their people and their environment. Both in our country and abroad, there are people who, if we could place in their hands the money, the tools, and the know-how, could get to work to improve their own lot and thus help us all with the greatest problem that confronts the human race.

It is not a question of pouring money down the drain; it is a question of the haves of the world being good Samaritans to the have-nots. And it must not stop with economic assistance. Money and food for all would not guarantee peace and international good will. Indeed, we need to expend our efforts on behalf of the cause of justice, liberation, and human fulfillment, and on the related themes of population and ecology, mutually with the peoples of the Third World.

Such an effort may fail of course, but what if it were doomed from the start? Could the followers of Jesus turn back from it on that account? Did not Jesus himself embark on a cause that led him, not to success, but the Cross? He devoted himself to the cause of the poor and needy, the sick and troubled of his world, against the advice of the religious establishment, and in the end that cause brought him to his own death. But that did not stop him and it should not stop us. It is better, even if the world should go down in destruction that the victors:

When the forts of folly fall,
Find thy body by the wall.

Besides, the story of Jesus does not end with the Cross. After the Cross comes the Resurrection. That, of course, is a miracle, but it is one which we are promised: "For as in Adam all die, so also in Christ shall all be made alive" (I Cor. 15:22). If ever the world needed a miracle, now is the time. Can we prepare to trust God to bring it to pass?

VI THINGS AS INHERITANCE

Sometimes, in some churches, when the offering is brought forward, the choir or the congregation sings a Beethoven chant setting of King David's words (I Chron. 29:14): "All things come of Thee, O Lord, and of Thine own have we given Thee." Like many worship words chanted, spoken, or sung, they sometimes become hard to hear. At any rate, it is hard for me to remember that all things come from God. I am more inclined to think of the things that I own as having come by the sweat of my back. I do not own much, to be sure: an acre of land, a house, and two tired cars. But I worked, and my wife worked, and we bought them, and we paid for them, and they are *ours*.

Or are they? Who really owns the land? At the county courthouse, there is a deed on file that shows I bought the land from someone, who bought it from someone, and so on back to the days when it was granted by the state to a farmer as part of a large tract. But where did the state get it? From the Indians? And, if it was theirs, where did they get it?

Or, to look at it another way, I own a great deal more than just one acre of land. Because I am an American, I own one two-hundred-millionth of the land owned by my country in the form of national parks, military bases, and courthouses. That means, if my figuring is correct, that along with you and each of my other fellow Americans, I own 700 million acres of land. I'm really a rich man. Or, if you want to push this idea to its logical extreme, we could say that we all own the whole world: billions of tons of sea water, acres of jungles and deserts, mountains, ice caps, and prairies, all to do with as we please. We own the whole earth and, now that we've planted our feet on it, the moon as well.

Or do we? A hundred ringing biblical affirmations say otherwise:

> The earth is the Lord's and the fulness thereof,
>   the world and those who dwell therein (Ps. 24:1).

> For God is the king of all the earth (Ps. 47:7).

> And he [God] has put all things under [Jesus']
>   his feet and has made him the head over all things
>   (Eph. 1:22).

The earth belongs to God, and any sense of ownership that we may have must be that of one who has received a gift. Thus Moses called Canaan "the good land which the Lord your God gives you for an inheritance." And that is a question that yet remains to be settled, judging from the situation in the Middle East at the present time. Who does own the land we call Israel? That nation, in its present form, has only existed since World War II. For centuries before that, the Arabs were there. Jews argue that it used to be their land by the gift of God; Arabs argue that even before that it was the property of *their* ancestors. Surely no happy solution will be found until all parties concerned remember that it is God's land, and they set about to use it for his glory and the common good of his people. But that is not so easy to decide. When Europeans settled Africa and America, they felt it was their right, as "civilized" people, to claim the undeveloped lands. In Africa now, nearly every nation has risen to claim that the land belongs to the native peoples, not the foreign interlopers. In America, where the Indian was effectively wiped out or confined, this has not happened to that extent. However, such events as that at Wounded Knee, S.D., (where the Sioux nation stood off the United States' government troops in 1973, searching for certain rights) serve to remind us that they might someday rise up. Would they be right or wrong?

Some countries operate under a principle which assigns ownership of property to the state, others with a system of private ownership, but in every case "things," both real and personal, are passed down from one generation to the next as a kind of inheritance. Thus we cannot truly say "this is mine." It also belongs to my children and their children. And what I do *with* it or *to* it will vitally affect their inheritance. The human race generally ignores this responsibility so that the old biblical saying becomes true again: "The fathers have eaten sour grapes, and the children's teeth are set on edge" (Jer. 31:29). This problem is becoming increasingly difficult for two main reasons.

One reason is the increasing mobility of the population. In the days when most people lived on a farm and passed that land on to their children, it was fairly simple to keep up the inheritance business until there got to be too many sons to share the land. For this reason some of them moved to new frontiers like the American west and establish new landed dynasties. But we are running out of land. And today people live not on farms, but in cities (this is true of 80 percent of Americans), and the average American moves more often than a minister! For that reason some ministers are now buying their own homes, since the turnover in real estate makes it thus possible for them to begin to build equity in a place to retire. If our people are increasingly moving from apartment to apartment or from house to house, it becomes harder and harder to think of things as permanently your own (except for money in the bank).

The other aggravation to the problem is the sheer size of the world's population. This is bringing about such an ecological crisis that, apart from the hunger problem dealt with in the last chapter, the very survival of the planet, our only home, is in question. Just listen to the paragraph headings from a December, 1970, *National Geographic* article on pollution:

Nature Operates in Precarious Balance
Hard Choice Faces Many Communities
Smog Shrouds Los Angeles; Tokyo Fights for Breath
Jet Planes Spew Tons of Water
Rivers Overwhelmed by Man's Wastes
Oil Fouls Troubled Waters
"Boundless" Seas Are Polluted, Too
DDT—Boon and Hazard
Strip Mines Ravage the Land
"Massive Debt to Our Environment"

The picture is alarming. I would only mention one way in which this problem affects me personally. For forty-five years I have been traveling every summer to the same spot in the mountains where my favorite view of the distant hills has always been. For the past five years, that view has been almost completely obscured, *even on sunny days,* by a thick haze in the air. I don't know about you, but I'm worried.

The troublesome thing is that we should have known we were responsible. We have been under orders since Adam to till the earth and take charge of it. And we have been told how God's concern is from generation to generation. But we have forgotten the meaning of a very important Bible word, and that is *stewardship.* We usually think of pledge time or canvass Sunday when we hear that word, but it really means a great deal more than just money. I am told that the word originated from an old English expression *sty ward,* meaning the "keeper of the pigs." From that lowly beginning, it came to refer to anyone who had responsibility for all his master's estates (see Luke 16:1-9). Eventually, the word became a proper name for a royal British family, and is found in our phone books, sometimes spelled Stuart and sometimes Stewart. From pig-keeper to a king's household is a long journey for a word. But it is a royal word for Christians and means that the keeping of common things is a royal task. Indeed, our care of the material world is a sacred task.

The biblical doctrine of the tithe, or tenth, is founded in a Hebrew rule which, like the sabbath commandment, was designed to help man remember that he is a part of the created universe. He returns a portion of it to God as a symbol of his recognition of his creaturehood. This in turn is used to finance the priesthood, in other words, to run the program of the church (see Deut. 14:22-29 and Num. 18:21-32). But this Hebrew rule was never intended to indicate that a legalistic gift of 10 percent was the end of man's duty. It is not true that 10 percent belongs to God and the rest belongs to me. The tithe was and is not a stewardship goal but a place of beginnings. Remember what Jesus said to the young man whose money was his god (Mark 10; see pp. 35-36). His orders involve God's ownership of every facet of the young man's life: his property and even his thoughts and deeds. Listen to the active verbs: "Go! Sell! Give! Come! Follow!" Jesus is saying that before happiness can be a reality for that young man and, indeed for any of us, God must be seen as sole and complete owner of the entire person. On another occasion, Jesus put it this way: "For whoever would save his life will lose it; and whoever loses his life for my sake, he will save it. For what does it profit a man if he gains the whole world and loses or forfeits himself" (Luke 9:24, 25)?

Perhaps at the time we are accustomed to make pledges to the church for the year ahead, it might be instructive to design a pledge card to include the giving of one's whole life. If you filled out such a card for your life, what would it include? Perhaps something like this?

I acknowledge that everything I am and have is a gift from God, and so I pledge in the coming year to return that gift to him.

I promise to take good care of the body that he has given me by eating regularly, getting proper rest, and exercising.

I promise to use my mind so that it will grow and be of value. I will study to understand and order my life. I will set free my creative talent and learn to live a rich life.

I will work hard and honestly at my job, trying to give to the world useful goods or service.

I will take care of the things that are mine, keeping them painted, cleaned, mowed, oiled, polished, stored, or straightened up. I will take care of the world of things by not wasting energy and by recycling my trash and avoiding the use of destructive products that might harm the environment.

I will give of my time to help my neighborhood, my family, my city, and my world in projects of brotherly and sisterly love. I will set aside _____ hours for service to others.

I will remember to smell the flowers, to enjoy the world, to sing, to dance, to laugh—and to praise God in the common things I do.
(And, oh yes, I'll give $_____ a week to my church.)

Such a declaration would be in keeping with the injunction of Paul in Romans 12:1: "to present your bodies as a living sacrifice, holy and acceptable to God, which is your spiritual worship." And it would certainly be a proper response to the beloved words in Isaac Watts' hymn:

> Were the whole realm of nature mine,
> That were an offering far too small;
> Love so amazing, so divine,
> Demands my soul, my life, my all.

It is unfortunately easy to fall into the trap of thinking that when we have given money we have given ourselves; but sometimes we use our money, or the things that money can buy, to bribe people so that we won't have to give ourselves. Have you ever heard a beleaguered parent say something like this: "I just don't understand that child. I have given her everything she ever wanted—clothes, money, a car—all the things I never had. But she never seems grateful for any of it." If so, perhaps you were tempted to reply, "Maybe you didn't give her the one thing that mattered: yourself and your love." But it is not for us to make that decision about another person. Instead, let's make it for ourselves. Are there ways in which you buy someone's affection with gifts or bribe them to keep their distance? This does not, of course, mean that gifts of things or money are bad. On the contrary, if I am unable to part with my money, that is probably a symbol that I am pretty tight-fisted with my love, too. It just means that money can never be a substitute for genuine love (see Matt. 5:23-24).

Perhaps in our taking of the offering on Sunday (see pp. 26-27), we could devise some way of reminding people through effective gesture or symbol that the giving of our money is really a symbol of self-giving. What would be a meaningful act to demonstrate this? Back in the fifties, most women's purses were fastened with little catches made of balls that clicked together. One Sunday when I was a very inexperienced pastor, I chided my ladies for making such a clicking noise during the silent prayer that preceded the offering. After church, a very wise woman got me aside and said, "Pastor, you'll never get anywhere in the ministry if you fuss at people for opening their pocketbooks! That is a sacramental noise. It is the sign of people dedicating themselves." I believe she is right, and maybe we can figure out some symbol. So many people nowadays give their money in the mail by check and just sit there when the plate is passed. What if, at the time of the offering, we all got up and went to the table, even those of us who have no money, and stood there as if to dedicate our whole being to the God who made us? On the way we could greet one another with the passing of the peace in an act of giving ourselves to one another, further symbolizing our stewardship. (Sometimes I think there is too much furniture in our churches, screwed to the floor so we can't move around very much. But on Communion Sunday we manage to come forward.) Maybe you and your pastor can come up with a way to express this best for your congregation. I don't really care what, but I hate to see the day coming when the symbolism of giving is lost, and instead of offering plates we pass out the credit card printing press for everybody to use!

But whether we devise an effective symbol or not, our task is clear. Stewardship is more than giving of money; it is a way of life. It is an attitude of respect for the world around us, and for the people who will live in it after we are gone. This is true for persons of all ages, but especially for those of us who are old enough to remember passing traditions and relay them on to the new generation coming. In a day when older people are feeling the pain of a sense of uselessness or loneliness, it might help for them to think of themselves as a very essential bridge between the generations gone and those to come. To children, it may seem that the resources of earth are inexhaustible; to older folk, who have seen the results of such things as erosion, faulty planning, and careless management, the gifts of nature are very precious. It is hard to get a true and accurate picture, and those who can remember will be of help to the rest of us.

Every vested interest seems to sing its own song and it is difficult for the average citizen to know whom to believe. As you can tell, if you stay around me very long, I am hooked on trees. I believe that Joyce Kilmer was right: only God can make one, and that they are one of his crowning achievements. And I often thank God that I live in North American which is (except for the Soviet Union) the most tree-full part of the world. But what is happening to our trees? Have we really learned the lesson from the indiscriminate logging of the last century? In *Time,* June, 1974, the American Forest Institute ran one of its "green paper" ads entitled, "'We're running out of trees:' The Great American Myth." It said, in part:

> A recent Gallup Poll shows most Americans think our forests are vanishing—that we're running out of trees.
> Fortunately, we aren't.
> True, civilization is encroaching on the forest, but we still have about 759 million acres of forestland.
> That's close to three-fourths of what was here when the Pilgrims landed.
>
> The good news is that we need never run out of forests—or wood products—in the United States. Not if we manage what we have wisely and continue to encourage involvement in forestry.
>
> So trees aren't like oil, or coal or even plastics. They're more like the storied cake: one we can eat and have, too.[1]

[1]*Time,* June 24, 1974, p. 41.

That is good news indeed. But does it tell the whole story? There may be as many acres of timber as there used to be, but how much of it is in young trees that may not be available for lumber for thirty to ninety years? And, in the meantime, what of our increasing demand for wood? In that same year, John J. Putman traveled the United States for *National Geographic* and wrote of the picture from the opposite point of view:

> The simple fact is, according to Forest Service analysis, that the supply of industry-owned softwood sawtimber on the Pacific Coast will decline substantially over the next thirty years. Industry has been cutting more wood than it has been growing. In the Douglas fir region, for instance, the harvests in recent years have been more than double the rate of growth.
>
> The reason: Industry is cutting old growth. These big volume trees can be felled in minutes, but producing replacements requires 50 to 100 years. Reforestation efforts, relatively recent, are not expected to close the gap.

I am not qualified to judge between these two opinions, so what do I do as an average citizen? A number of specific steps are open to me:

1. I can endeavor to be as conserving as possible in my own use of wood. The trees in my yard shed thousands of dead twigs each winter. Instead of hauling them off to junk yard, which is easier, I should chop them into neat kindling lengths and use them in my fireplace rather than buy kindling.

2. I can follow the advice of Smokey the Bear and take good care of the forests through which I travel or camp. It is certainly true that I can prevent *some* forest fires.

3. I can teach my children to love, know, and

71

appreciate trees; to tell a sugar maple from a silver maple, or a walnut from a pecan. Trees are like people. When you get to be good friends with them, you find they are as different as individuals can be and you learn to care about them.

4. I can refrain from wasting wood-produced articles: paper, matches, grocery bags, cellophane, boxes, and some plastics.

In short, I can begin to love the trees that God has made, and that in itself will produce my small help, but, beyond that, my enthusiasm for the cause will be a "good infection" to those around me, and, little by little, our combined efforts will begin to make a difference.

But trees are not necessarily your thing. In that case, let me and the other tree lovers worry about them. But at least do not let your greed or desire for "progress" run over the persons to whom the trees are important. The truth is, if it were not for their marvelous factory which converts carbon dioxide into oxygen, we would all soon die on a barren planet. But there is fragile beauty all around us in other things than trees. It is to the stewardship of all these things that we are called. All the earth belongs to God—"the cattle on a thousand hills"—and thus it is placed in trust for all of us, ours to use as an inheritance for the good of our brothers and sisters, and our children and grandchildren. In some ways this is a monumental and complex task, involving all the skills that education, government, and industry can muster. But in other ways it is a very simple thing, involving a basic attitude in each of us, namely that we follow from now on the adage, "Don't walk so fast that you cannot smell the flowers."

If we can come to the place where that is our attitude, then a life-style that could change history would belong to us. Instead of being in such a hurry to change the course of rivers or bring a new textile mill into our county, we might spend our time getting acquainted with the small folk of our gardens and yards: box turtles, frogs, and inchworms. We might plant a window box. We might clear and put to use a vacant lot. We might spend some time at the boys' club, conserving and nurturing that most precious of all natural resources. We might slip off some weekend with a canoe, just to paddle a lazy river and listen to the birds and smell the flowers for a change.

If we do that, we will see some things that disturb us: old automobiles rusting in the creek beds, ice boxes dumped along the banks, tires, six-pack rings, plastic milk cartons, aluminum cans, and chicken feathers littering the place. When we do see these things, we will know that we are a part of a sick world—a world that has forsaken the ancient command of God to subdue the earth. Instead we have wasted it, slopped around in it, and piled it full of junk until it looks like my bedroom looked when I was fourteen years old. I can clearly hear the voice of my mother saying, "You clean that mess up before you do another thing, do you hear?" And I wonder if that is not the voice of all our mothers, of Mother Nature, and of God himself, calling to the human race and asking us to set things straight before it is too late. Perhaps then will come to pass the good day foretold by Amos (9:14-15):

"I will restore the fortunes of my people Israel,
    and they shall rebuild the ruined cities and inhabit them;

they shall plant vineyards and drink their wine,
    and they shall make gardens and eat their fruit.
I will plant them upon their land,
    and they shall never again be plucked up
out of the land which I have given them,"
    says the Lord your God.

VII THE RHYTHM OF LIFE

"Remember the sabbath day, to keep it holy. Six days you shall labor, and do all your work; but the seventh day is a sabbath to the Lord your God; in it you shall not do any work . . ." (Exod. 20:8-10). Somewhere along the line we fell into the habit of naming the days of the week after heavenly bodies and Norse gods. It's really too bad, because nobody ever thinks of them as Sun's day, Moon's day, Woden's day, etc. They are just names. If you're like me, you probably tend to think of Monday as the first day of the week since that's when the work and school schedules begin. Indeed, Sunday, which is really the first day, is considered by most Americans as part of the "weekend" rather than the week's beginning. Maybe it's time to rename the days of the week so that they can reflect once again the ancient rule which the seven-day cycle helps us to follow: humankind needs to live in harmony with the rhythm of life. What would you call the days if you were naming them now? I believe I would want to opt for at least two names that the Spanish use because they help preserve both the Hebrew sabbath and the Christian day of Resurrection celebration. Saturday is *Sabbado:* the sabbath; and Sunday is *Domingo,* the Lord's day. But whatever we call them, our days need to be used in a healthy pattern of work, rest, and play.

The really disturbing thing about the breakdown of the so-called "blue laws" in America is the danger that many people will lose the blossoming out that enforced weekends make possible. It is good to see people freed from superstitious adherence to "rules" for their own sake, but we had better be careful not to throw out the baby with the bath water. According to Genesis 2:2-3, God himself participates in the kind of rhythm we are describing so it seems that we who are made in his image are to follow the same pattern. To suppose that we can do it better than our Creator is the utmost blasphemy. Perhaps that is the reason that of the Ten Commandments, this one goes into the most detail. At any rate, since the beginning it has been the most debated and discussed of the rules, and the one subject to the most nit-picking. What constitutes work? In the most orthodox of the legalistic Hebrew schools, the rabbis held that if you carried a chair from one side of the room to another in order to sit by a window to read, that would not be work; but if you dragged it, causing the legs to plow furrows in the dirt floor, that would be plowing which is a sabbath violation. A tailor who accidentally left a needle stuck in his garment would be "carrying the tools of his trade" on the holy day. In order to determine how far travel could be done on the sabbath, the rabbis announced that a certain distance would be a legitimate sabbath day's journey; beyond that, no one should venture away from his own property. A way of getting around this was devised by those who absolutely *had* to make such a trip: during the week before, they might carry a few stones from the wall of their homes, placing them at suitable intervals along the intended route, so that never would they have to go more than a sabbath's journey from their own property. Absurd? Well, yes, because the deep meaning of sabbath had been forgotten by the worthy scribes.

Jesus was well aware of the gnat-straining and it became the focal point of many of his clashes with the religious power structure of his day. Look at the incidents recorded by Mark in 2:23—3:6. Note that the behavior of his disciples was not what you or I would call "work." They were simply picking grain as they walked, and eating it raw. But the Pharisees saw this as a technical violation of the rules. Apparently, in what was at that time only a short association with their master, the disciples had already absorbed something of his free spirit and were able to commit this misdemeanor. Immediately they were criticized. (It isn't surprising; we read in Mark 3:2 that they were out to get them, just waiting for the first slipup.) In response, Jesus told the pharisees a story they well knew, that of David eating the holy bread in the temple. "The sabbath was made for man," he said, "not man for the sabbath." But we ought not to conclude from that verse that thereby any man can do whatever he pleases on the sabbath. For Jesus goes on to announce, "So the Son of man is lord even of the sabbath." You can bet that this was a disturbing reply to the Pharisees. They were already upset with Jesus for his associations and his behavior (see Gen. 2:15-22). Now he is claiming to have authority over and above the law.

But this is to misread Jesus altogether. It is very important to get it straight that he did not come to destroy the law, but to fulfill it (Matt. 5:17). Radical reform of the religious life of man does not consist in kicking over the old and replacing it with something new. Indeed, the word *radical* means just the opposite: going to the roots. Jesus was out-conserving the conservative Pharisees. They were interested in the jot and tittle of the law (that is the crossing of "t's" and the dotting of "i's"), while he went straight to the heart of the matter. Remember how, in the Sermon on the Mount, he moved from talking about the outward crimes of murder and adultery to the inward sins of hatred and lust? Jesus' law is really much tougher than the law of the Pharisees. They want men to keep the rules; Jesus wants them to be born again! And so he is returning our thoughts to the original meaning of the sabbath buried in antiquity: it was not created to lay a burden of rules on us but to give us a regular routine in life of stopping to smell the flowers so that we can learn to blossom ourselves.

The next incident makes it even more clear. This time Jesus' activity was not picking corn but healing a sick man. The gallery was full of hecklers, just waiting for him to commit a healing so that they could accuse him of a violation of the fourth commandment. It wouldn't have taken a mind reader to see that, and with all his perception Jesus could tell exactly what they were up to. So he stole their thunder. Before helping the man, he looked around at everybody assembled there and asked, "What is the right thing to do on the sabbath: healing or hurting?" And they wouldn't answer because of course they couldn't. And this hurt Jesus so much and made him so angry that without another word to the crowd, he turned and spoke to the sick man and healed him. And, as Mark records, the Pharisees went out and immediatel got together with the political power structure to figure out how to get this Jesus. Why were they so upset? Because they had a neat system all figured out in which they were comfortable, and they had built a livelihood in explaining to people how to keep the rules; now they all seem to be overthrown by a man whose claim is an astonishing one: the sabbath was not made for rules but for making man whole. (Note here the beautiful relationship between the words *whole* and *holy, holiday,* and *holy day*. The sabbath is a day for making men whole again. A similar relationship exists between the medical ointment, *salve*, and the spiritual state called *salvation*.)

It is sad that the negative interpretation of sabbath observance has so permeated the Christian church. The day that was meant for rejoicing has been thereby reduced to a day for grumbling. This can be illustrated by taking a group of Christians of all ages and asking them to draw a picture of the earliest memory they have of going to church. Some of the pictures will be cheerful and sunshiny with lots of smiles, but a large proportion of them will contain stern, frowning preachers or large ominous mammas with "shhhhh!" being the most prominent word remembered. Church is thus a stifling experience, rather than the liberating adventure it was meant to be. Children from an early age tend to misquote Psalm 122:1 to read, "I was *mad* when they said to me, 'Let us go to the house of the Lord!'" And when they get a little older, given the opportunity to escape, they will flee the scene always with a feeling of loss so that they will think, "I was *sad* when they said . . . " The only way to get the gladness back again is to become once again as a child (Mark 10:15) with all the openness, honesty, and wonder that childhood entails. You see, Christians worship not on Saturday, the night of rest, the dark time while Christ lay in the tomb, but on the first day of the week: The Lord's day—the day of Resurrection! It has no business being a bad day. It must be a good day. It is a day for blossoming, for rejoicing, for coming alive, for dancing, for singing and celebrating. And when we make it into a heaviness, we are celebrating death, not life.

What is a good way for Christians to spend the Lord's day? Here's a list that seems good to me:

—Gather with the church to celebrate. I put that first because it is our inherited pattern from the New Testament and because I don't think we can keep up the rhythm of life without gathering to be fed by one another. Nobody can keep on celebrating alone, not in this hostile world.

—Plant a garden.

—Take a canoe trip with the family.

—Hunt for arrowheads. (Then leave them where you found them for the next persons who come along! Same goes for throwing back the fish. Wasn't it Thoreau who wondered, "Who hears the fishes when they cry?"

—Visit some person you have always wanted to get to know.

—Take a hot meal to somebody.

—Listen to a symphony, a rock concert, or a folk mass.

—Write a poem. It doesn't have to be heavy or even rhyme. It could be Haiku, Japanese poetry of three lines giving a feeling or thought about nature. There should be seventeen syllables divided into five, seven, five.

THE RHYTHM OF LIFE

A cool cucumber.
I eat it on a hot day,
Like spring in my mouth.

—Design your dream house with someone you love.
—Take a long walk or ride.
—Find three other persons and be a quartet.
—Paint a picture, carve wood, weave a basket, bake ceramics, or weld some scrap metal sculpture. If you don't know how, get a book from the library and learn how.
—Call your mother on the phone.
—Learn the names of all the trees on your block.
—Build a birdhouse.
—Rope off the street (get permission) and have a block party with all the neighbors you've never really met.
—Take your wife on a date.
—Scrape together all the spare money you can find in pockets, dresser drawers, etc. Add something from everybody's allowance and, when you get the total, hold a family conference to decide how to spend it. One Sunday give it all away; another Sunday, spend it on something special for the family.
—Make a fish chowder.
—Write a litany of thanksgiving.
—Make a resolution for Monday morning, something that you really should have done long ago.
—Say your prayers and go to bed.

Well, that's a plenty. Make your own list. Remember that it should be list not of have-to but of get-to. Not things that you are obligated to do, but things that you have always wanted to do or thought you should. It should be a day of blossoming or of turning from a caterpillar into a butterfly.

Whatever your work schedule, it is an absolute must that you get a regular sabbath; that is, time to do your own personal thing, to be renewed, to remember the Resurrection. If you do not, then you will surely die. The commandments which we break kill us, not because God is vindictive, but because they are laws like the law of gravity. When we violate them, we do not actually break them—we break ourselves against them. And one of the things the sabbath law means is: You die unless you have rest and re-creation (or recreation).

But it isn't enough simply to take time off. It must be time well spent. Creative use of leisure time is essential for growth, family solidarity, and ultimate happiness. I confess that I am not a very good counselor on this subject for I have never had enough leisure time in which to do all the things I want to do. When I take time off from writing this book, I have a novel I want to finish. And when I get time off from that, I have a room I want to add on the house. And so on. But I understand that there are many people who don't know what to do with their time. If so, I can make some recommendations:

Get in touch with the community agencies: Boy and Girl Scouts, Big Brothers, Red Cross, Mental Health Association, Hospital Auxiliary, etc. They need you!

Contact your local night-school branch of the state university or college near your town. They probably have classes in something you would like to learn. In my town there are classes in song writing, fiddle playing, banjo picking, and arc welding. Someday I will get around to them.

Your church can use you.

But before you ask somebody else to tell you how to use your time, take this simple test with yourself. Make a list of the fifty most interesting things that ever happened to you—good and bad. Think back to your childhood, adolescence, early and later adult years. When you finish that list, does it suggest to you that you are the sort of person who likes to do certain things? If not, go through and cross out all the things that don't have anything to do with vocation, such as the day your first child was born, etc. Then if it still doesn't speak to you, narrow it down to the ten or twelve most important ones. When you look at that list, can you fill in these blanks:

I am a _____ person who likes to _____.
(When I took this test I discovered that: "I am a wordy person who likes to work alone." So I became a writer for my second vocation.) If you are already working full time at something you don't like, this test can also be used to help you find out what you might really like to change to. It isn't too late.

Redistributing the weekly cycle of living to make sure that we have a healthy sabbath, a time for renewal and blossoming, can be a lifesaver. But we ought also to make sure that the yearly schedule has good healthy vacations in it for study, play, and discovery. Nothing is better calculated to help us remember our relationship to the material world than to camp out in it. And we in America are the most blessed people in the world. The choice is yours. You can take a chrome-plated motor home if you want to, or you can take a back-pack into Yosemite or the Great Smokies for four dollars a day. But you don't have to go camping—go to a lodge or motel. Buy a ticket on the bus that lets you ride anywhere in the United States for so many days. Travel abroad, but remember that you are a missionary wherever you go, so don't act like an ugly American. Touch the earth; keep a scrapbook of photos or do like my grandmother who brought a rock from everywhere she visited and built them into a fireplace! If you work at a job from which you don't get a vacation, then you're in the wrong line of work! If you are retired, and think you are on a perpetual vacation and can't think of anything to do, then *you're* in the wrong line of work! To believe in God is to believe that he did not make a mistake when he created you! He has a use for you, you are a useful person in his kingdom even if you think you are too old, sick, crippled, ugly, or ignorant to do anything. There is no such thing as a useless person. I cannot prescribe for you by the book, but I can guarantee to you that your use is there and commend you to search for it. If the sort of device I mentioned doesn't work, then go to your pastor, a vocational guidance counselor, or other qualified person, and ask for help. They'll be glad to see you.

In most churches we celebrate the changing of the seasons by changing the emphases of the church year. In your household or family you can lift the spirits of yourselves, and get closer to the changing of the material world from winter to spring, by celebrating those seasons in the home. Here are some suggestions:

Make an Advent wreath (for the four weeks preceding Christmas) using, if you like, four purple candles for each of the Sundays and one white one for Christmas Eve. Have special family worship each week built around the lighting of the candles.

Try not to sing carols during Advent—hold off as long as you can so that you don't get bored with them and then have a huge carol sing on Christmas Eve. (Remember that the Hebrews began celebrating their holidays the night before, so for us Judeo-Christians, Christmas really begins at sundown on Christmas Eve. Remember, too, that it lasts *twelve* days.)

Cut down on the lighting to save energy and make lots of your own decorations for inside the house. From soda straws tied together with thread you can make a great star. Or you can make things from old magazines, pine cones, aluminum soft drink cans, glitter, and glue. Many magazines will have a section on this around Christmas.

Skip the Christmas cards this year and save the money for something special. (The best reward will be not having to bother with this hassle.)

Instead of giving a glut of gifts on Christmas morning, spread out the gift-sharing over the twelve days of Christmas. (No partridges in pear trees; that wouldn't help the ecology if we cut down the pears. Come to think of it, though, if you planted them . . .)

For Lent, make a real sacrifice that will do some real good. I mean give up alcohol or cigarettes if they are a problem to you. But beyond that, do something positive, like deciding to drop by to see a certain invalid once a week, or devoting yourself to an ecological problem, or picking a civic duty that is being neglected and get started organizing it.

For Easter, plan a celebration sure enough. Hire a hall for a dance. If your church doesn't want to hold a dance, hold one yourself! Think of ways in which the truth of our risen Lord can really be brought home, not simply in words but in deed. Let the children take part in the planning and let the teen-agers do their thing. If you don't have any musicians in the neighborhood, get a record player, or at least a tambourine. Have a ball. Sing the old songs and the new ones. The new humanity is surely coming. Why not begin now?

VIII TOWARD A CHRISTIAN BUDGET

I hate to tackle this chapter because I hate budgets. But if this book is to make any sense at all, it will have to do so in terms of the daily details that make up life. And though budgets are chores, in the long run they set us free. Even with a good budget, the ends never seem to meet. But that's the point! Budgets aren't for making ends meet. Money isn't an end. Budgets are for making *means* fall into line! The ends we want are what Paul calls the fruits of the Spirit: "love, joy, peace, patience, kindness, goodness, faithfulness, gentleness, self-control" (Gal. 5:22-23). A budget won't buy them, but governing our money wisely may free us to find them.

Let's begin with what we'll give away. If you wait until you have paid for everything else and then start looking for leftovers to share, there won't be any. But if you start with your gifts, by an amazing miracle you will almost always find that there is enough left over to meet the necessities. (I didn't believe that either until I tried it on a dare with myself, but it does work.) Okay, what percentage of my money shall I give? All Christians know the word *tithe*, which simply means 10 percent. But to some the word has a hateful sound. Let's face it, a tithe from one person is harder than a tithe from another. If you made three thousand dollars a year (which is *thirty* times as much as most of the world's people make!) a tithe of three hundred dollars might mean shoes or beans for children who otherwise might go hungry or barefoot. But if you made $300,000.00 a year, you could probably squeak by fairly well on the $270,000.00 left over after the tithe. In fact, tax-wise, you would be better off to increase your giving to charitable causes. So we just can't say: Make it an automatic 10 percent and let it go. What do you do then? Why not take a hard look at what you are actually giving now. What is it? Two percent of your gross income? Five percent? You know a lot of us got into the habit of putting a quarter into the plate when our parents gave it to us as children, and we're still operating at that level. Now set yourself a goal of increasing it a little (maybe one or two percentage points a year) until you get to a place that you honestly consider a sacrificial level. Don't stop at 10 percent. I know a family that puts aside 30 percent of their income into a special bank account each month. At the end of the month, they take pleasure in writing a check for 10 percent to their church, another 10 percent to regular causes in their community, and (here's the best part), they save the third portion to build up interest until something really special comes along. Then they have a family council and decide how to spend it. Can you imagine how much more fun it is to decide what to do with a surplus than to have the usual squabble over what to trim?

But never mind about what the Joneses are doing. You and I have to establish our own budgets, not somebody else's. And no simple formula will work. The tithe means 10 percent. But is that 10 percent to the church, or 10 percent to all charitable causes? And do I take it off before or after income taxes? The answer is none of these things. That figure of 10 percent, which used to be a legal obligation on the ancient Hebrews, is still a good starting point for Christian giving, but it isn't the end we seek. To give the whole tithe to the church, after taxes, would merely be a duty fulfilled and no grounds for glory (see Luke 17:10). We can't stop there. Like the rich young man, we have to go the whole way (Mark 10:21). Look back at the pledge we made (pp. 66-67). Does the amount budgeted to give away reflect a giving of the whole self?

Now then, what do we do with the rest? Of course there are some things that are going to come as sure as time and tide. They are death and taxes. Some money must be set aside to cover the bill when it arrives. I have always been grateful for a paternalistic government that withholds my tax money and my social security so that I won't have to face the ides of April with empty pockets. But nobody is withholding money to pay for my funeral or my wife's or that of the children. So we have an insurance policy to take care of that. Burying somebody is not all that expensive if you don't want it to be. If, as a Christian, you believe in the Resurrection, then what happens to the physical body is not especially important. (For that matter, why should it be important to a pagan?) A memorial association can help you finance a funeral for very little. And a medical school might help you do it for nothing.

After we have allowed for dying, we have to have somewhere to live. But do you have to live *where* you live? If, like many Americans, you are stuck because of your job in an unhappy corner of a big city, I don't know what to suggest. It's unfortunate to be trapped like that. I can only say there is still land available in the country where you might build a log house and get away from the noise if that suits you. But as for the middle American, we seem forever to be looking for a little bigger, a little fancier house. It really is nice to live in posh surroundings. I would certainly like to have a swimming pool, or even a large flagstone patio and membership in a community pool. But the question is this: Are you the master or is the house? I'm not saying that it is impossible for anyone who lives in a big house to get into the kingdom of heaven; I'm only saying it's easier for a camel to go through a needle's eye (Mark 10:25). In other words, only by the grace of God can it be done (Mark 10:27). Blessed is the man whose house is a home, not a great heavy load pressing down upon his back. There are alternatives to houses: apartments, condominiums, retirement homes, communes, mobile homes—even hotel rooms. Are you in the one that suits you best?

Next comes food. As this is being written, food prices are sky-rocketing. Maybe they will be down again by the time it gets into print, but I doubt it. It doesn't usually work that way. But there are ways to save money.[1] For instance, how many utensils do you have in the kitchen? If you really back into the corner, about all you absolutely have to have to cook with is a pot, a sharp knife, and a can opener. After that, everything is a matter of

[1] There are plenty of good paperback books and government pamphlets (which are free) that can help you cut corners. I've enjoyed a delightful paperback book called *How to Live Cheap but Good* by Martin Poriss, Dell Publishing Company, $1.50.

convenience. Sound crazy? Well, maybe so if you're pretty well-off, but what if you have to choose between an electric skillet and an extra pair of shoes? Which is more important? And more than that, which would you rather have, an electric carving knife or thirty-five dollars to give away to somebody who is in need? Nobody can answer that but you. Certainly we don't need everything that plugs up all the drawers in our kitchens. Beyond that, there are thousands of ways to save money on food. Here are just a handful:

—Trade where they don't give trading stamps.
—Eat good marinated round steak rather than ribeye. (It has less fat anyway.)
—Be careful to read and compare the weight and volumes stated on packages.
—Grow your own vegetables (and meat).
—Buy in quantity and keep a freezer. (Don't try this unless you are really good at planning and budgeting. It could cost you more in the long run.)
—Make judicious use of leftovers.
—Drink water with meals—it's cheap and good for you.

Then I would put clothing down as the next essential. Maybe if our first parents hadn't fouled things up so, we wouldn't be in that bind at all, though some scientists seem to think another ice age is on the way—maybe in the next 100,000 years. In that case, even without the modesty question, we'll need clothes. But will they have to be *stylish*? What percentage of the cost of clothes is due to the label in the lining? In this day of relaxed dress codes for women and men alike, you can buy whatever looks good to you and it doesn't matter a fig whether everybody else thinks it's stylish or not. You can even drop by the dry cleaners and purchase clothing that has been forgotten and abandoned there. Too much for your dignity? Who would ever know? And, really now, what if they did—wouldn't you come off rather cleverly? Also, learn to do your own dry cleaning. That can save a good bit.

Then there is the matter of transportation. This will of course depend on how far you live from where you need to be, and on what public facilities are available. But here is my list of means of transportation listed in order of expense from the cheapest to the most expensive:

> walking
> bicycling
> city bus or train
> motorbike
> used car
> rental or leased car
> taxi
> owning an expensive car
> owning two cars
> owning three cars and a motor home

Where do you come on that list? There are other possibilities, of course, including car pools, but the one that involves the most physical movement on your part is the one that is best for you and also the cheapest. Why do we take the luxury way out? Ask yourself how far you are willing to walk. It would even be economical and healthier if you could drive to a convenient parking place, then walk the rest of the way to work. You'll get to know people and your city better, I can guarantee!

Then there is education. I am told that scholarships go unused every year and that there are still fields where skill shortages exist. If you are very poor, there are various government agencies that can help provide you with the necessary training to learn a trade. If you are middle income, you can learn a second vocation or a creative, useful hobby skill at many of our good night-school extensions of state universities. Do you have to send your children to the fanciest private school in town? There may be a good reason why a child with special gifts or needs might want such attention, but there is also real educational value in going to a school where you rub shoulders with all sorts and conditions of people and classes. Public education, the cheapest available, can be superior to the private kind.

You can save money on health care! The simplest and best way is to eat well, sleep well, and get plenty of exercise. This alone will decrease your need for medical help by a considerable amount. Also avoid alcohol, tobacco, and other luxuries known to be dangerous to good health. See your dentist regularly. Purchase drugs by "generic" rather than brand names at discount drug stores. Have an annual checkup with a family doctor (you can still find them some places). Purchase the most economical health insurance plan, if this is not provided where you work.

Celebrate! This paragraph is related to the preceding one. You should save enough money to spend it occasionally on something really fun and liberating—a trip, a piece of family recreational equipment, a special meal with everybody's favorites. We know that in the life of Jesus there were times when he was not at all "aescetic." Indeed, the leaders of the people were upset with his life-style. They called him "a glutton and a drunkard, a friend of tax collectors and sinners!" (Matt. 11:19). The best story about what Paul Tillich calls "holy waste," is in Mark 14:3-9. It is the lovely tale of the woman who broke the expensive jar and poured the costly ointment on Jesus' head. It may have been worth several hundred dollars in our inflationary economy. It was probably Judas, the treasurer of the band of disciples, who was so upset over this. At any rate, right after this, he went out and made plans to betray Jesus (10:11). It is the only recorded time that Jesus called anyone "beautiful." "You always have the poor with you," he said, and added, in effect, "You should always be taking offerings for them: but some times are special." This is the last incident which Mark records before the upper room and the beginning of the passion story. I can't help feeling that in speaking of this ointment poured out that Jesus is thinking of his own young life, about to be wasted, with nothing to claim for his ministry but a few confused and frightened disciples. But some things are worth dying for, and on the humble scale, sometimes families or individuals ought to "blow a little bread" on some pure fun.

In short, check to see if the way we spend our money is an honest expression of the beliefs we profess:

1. In the first place, we need ask of every item in our budget: can we celebrate it? That is, can we in good conscience offer it on the altar of God as something worthy of a gift to him?

2. Do we really need it? Our attic is jammed full of things we once thought we really needed. Remember the

style of life our Lord led: "Foxes have holes, and birds of the air have nests; but the Son of man has nowhere to lay his head" (Luke 9:58).

3. Is it *quality* goods (or services)? Often it is false economy simply to buy the cheapest thing we can find. From shirts to stocks we need to check the merchandise and determine if it is something really worth having. (I am typing this manuscript on a fairly expensive electric typewriter, but I can tell you it is a money saver! It is dependable and fast [although it doesn't spell very well], and I have it under a maintenance contract which services it every year. What I have saved in blood, sweat, tears, and lost time has paid for its initial cost many times over. And every time I sit down at it, it gives me a good feeling. It is a familiar thing that I love and appreciate. I think maybe I have an I-thou relationship with a Smith-Corona!)

4. Can we afford it? I deliberately didn't put this question first because it isn't always the most important. Not, Is there money enough in the bank? but in the long run, when all our other debts are in, Will this one put us further in the hole or will we still have our heads above water? Sometimes a thing or event may be so valuable to us that we will want to make considerable sacrifice to obtain it (see Matt. 13:44-46). The question is: Have we weighed it against our other hopes and dreams?

5. If we lose it, will it destroy us? We should never become so attached to anything that its loss would be the end of the world. If I have a passion for anything like that, I'd really do better without it. Basically Jesus said that it is better to lose your right hand or your eye, than to have them destroy you (see Matt. 5:29-30).

IX GOD'S NOMADS

Because I love the church I hesitate to fuss at her, but by the same token because I love her, I have to be straight with her. Of all the places in the world where things ought to be in their proper perspective, it ought to be where the people of God gather. But I'm afraid this isn't always the case. From the front door of the church where I worship I can see five other steeples of other denominations. Each of us has a large house for worship which is used for about three hours weekly. (I don't much like the word *sanctuary* because it means a "holy place" which is a sort of denial of what this book is about, namely that all God's creation is holy). The rest of the time it is sitting there being heated or air-conditioned. Now, why couldn't we get together and schedule something like this:

> Jews: Saturday
> Lutherans: 8 to 10 on Sunday
> Presbyterians: 11 to 1 on Sunday
> Roman Catholics: 2 to 4 on Sunday
> Methodists: 5 to 7 on Sunday

Or we could each take a day. Or on non-special Sundays we could all use it at the same time!

Or look at it another way. How precious is our property

to us? Are church doors usually locked? If they are, what does this say to poor transients, especially in the wintertime, who might find a place of shelther on a pew. The usual response to this suggestion is fear of theft or vandalism, but how does that relate to Matthew 5:19-21? And, above all, does it sustain the eternal invitation in Matthew 11:28 "Come to me, all who labor and are heavy laden, and I will give you rest"? Granted, these are not simple questions; every church, like every individual Christian, has to face up to them. If we do not, then our decisions will be made for us by popular trends, styles in architecture that are "in," and whatever status symbols have the most vogue with people at the moment.

In I Kings 7, as part of the description of the magnificent temple that Solomon erected in Jerusalem, we are told that "upon the tops of the pillars was lily-work" (Verse 22). Lily-work is completely non-functional, like architectural "gingerbread." It may be beautiful but it doesn't help hold up the roof. For that matter, vessels of wood, pewter or plastic will hold water as well as vessels of gold (see verses 48-50). Why should offering plates be made of silver or brass when baskets might be better? So long as we are using them for glad celebration and for beauty that gives God the glory, then architectural extras can be a good thing. But whenever they become ends in themselves, that is, when we say "It really isn't church without those columns", we are in the kind of trouble that destroys worship: "I hate, I despise your feasts, and I take no delight in your solemn assemblies. Even though you offer me . . . offerings, I will not accept them. Take away from me the noise of your songs; to the melody of your harps I will not listen.

But let justice roll down like waters, and righteousness like an everflowing stream" (Amos 5:21-24). Whenever worship becomes a block to our social consciences and we neglect to feed the hungry, establish justice, or praise with gladness, lily-work loses its beauty; indeed, it can become an obscenity (Matt. 25:31-46 and I Cor. 13).

Just once, I would like to see a church organized with the following statement built into its initial commitment: *We will not build anything we do not need.* (It probably ought also to add, "or anything ugly or more expensive than we can afford.") I wonder how little we could get by on if we really tried. For example, why couldn't we worship and eat in the same room? Apparently the Christians at Corinth had the Lord's supper in connection with their common meal on the Lord's day and went right on with their prophesying and preaching (see I Cor. 11-14). What if, on the usual Sunday, a covered dish supper was included as part of the regular worship service, combining the two Jewish traditions from which we inherit our worship practices: the synagogue service of the word and the family service of the common meal? But whether they are combined or not, couldn't they take place in the same space? And how large should the space be? Huge, vaulted areas suggest cathedral-like atmosphere and perhaps reverence. But you can get that from tall tulip trees or pines. Why not meet out-of-doors from time to time? As for educational space, why couldn't our living rooms be used instead of all-electric classrooms on the public school model? I'm just asking.

How much money should a church spend on itself? You might want to get your annual budget and look at it, dividing it into the following major sections:

Building fund
Program expenses (salaries, equipment, upkeep)
Local charities and concerns
Denominational causes (churchwide)

How do the percentages shape up? What is the ideal?
Naturally this will vary from one church to the next, just
as the tithe question is related to the relative strength of
the individual family's income. But given the fact that in
each case it must be different, does your church have a
goal, such as 50 percent for a local program and 50
percent for others? And are you trying to raise it a little
each year as you move from your present position toward
that ideal?

In a sense, the church is a part of the world of things.
Of course it is: buildings, budgets, books, vestments,
musical instruments, bread, wine, water. All these things
are part of the church which is definitely *in* the world
(John 17:18). But there is also a sense in which the
church is not *of* the world (John 17:14). People are more
than bodies and our relationships with one another
create the true church. The quorum is two or three
(Matt. 18:20) and the actual material goods needed for
survival are few: "Take no gold, nor silver, nor copper in
your belts, no bag for your journey, nor two tunics, nor
sandals, nor a staff" (Matt. 10:9). St. Augustine taught
that we must say of every single thing in the world: "This
also is Thou," meaning that there is a part of God in every
created thing but that we must also say of every single
thing, "Neither is this Thou," for nothing (no thing) can
ever contain God. Yet the church, insofar as it is made up
of *persons* whose Lord is Jesus of Nazareth, can in a

sense contain God. This is an incredible mystery, but it is the audacious hope for the church for which Paul prayed: "that you may be filled with all the fulness of God" (Eph. 3:19). The secret mystery of life which Jesus came to teach us and which from our worldly perspective we find almost impossible to hear is this: The smaller can contain the larger. Or, to find your life you have to give it up. "For thus says the high and lofty One who inhabits eternity, whose name is Holy: 'I dwell in the high and holy place, and also with him who is of a contrite and humble spirit.'" (Isa. 57:15). Because we are *in* the world and because we do have secular tasks to perform, there is a proper place for *things* in the life of the church but there is no room for man's pomp or splendor. The glory belongs to God.

Now I want to let you in on a very dangerous secret. Once we can get hold of the concept that *things* were given to us to be given away, we will become a rich church. (For true riches, see I Cor. 9:2, 9 and Luke 12:21, 16:11.) It is hard to get persons to see this, but once seen it can work a miracle in the life of a congregation. Be warned, however, that there is a catch to it: if you deliberately try to lose your life, knowing that if you lose it you will find it, and your motive is not loss but gain, then it may not work, anymore than other forms of insincerity. But f you will really set about to give yourself away, a miracle will happen: bread cast upon waters has a way of returning (Eccles. 11:1). Let me illustrate. A certain church was in the spiritual doldrums. They were squabbling among themselves, attendance was off at worship and at church school (Isn't it always?) and the every-member canvass was falling far short of the expected goal. Some of the members were prayerfully discussing these unhappy conditions and one of them voiced the opinion, "I guess we've just bled everybody to the point where they have no more to give." At this point a wise person entered the conversation saying, "No, we have never given them the chance to learn the meaning of sacrifice." As a result of this, a decision was made not to cut back on the amount of money to be raised but to multiply it by two! Then meetings were held to enable the congregation to set goals for giving the money away: mission overseas, care for the needy in their hometown, recreation for children, medical and nursing care. Not only did they meet their goals, but interest and enthusiasm increased and the regular stewardship needs of the church were effectively carried out. The secret? "It is more blessed to give than to receive (Acts 20:35)."

This does not mean that preoccupation with material things is all wrong. What it does mean is that genuine participation in the down-to-earth work of the church is what gives people a sense of being and belonging. It is a clue to what is wrong with every aspect of the church's life, especially worship. We're like people working on an assembly line who cannot see the finished product at the end. No wonder the job is boring! We need to be artisans, working in wood, leather, or metal at a level where we can take pride and satisfaction in what we have created. Hired mourners cannot take the place of my own need to grieve. And I dare not hire professionals to be the church for me.

Not too long ago I was speaking in a church in the midwest when it suddenly dawned on me that it was a congregation divided by the chancel steps into two congregations! The pastor and I in our robes and the choir in their vestments and the minister of music were in the holy of holies, like costumed actors on a stage, while the rest of the people sat and watched us do the worshiping. Occasionally we let them sing along with the hymns, but otherwise they were not worshipers. They were spectators at a performance. I wanted badly to take off my robe and fling it to somebody on the fifth pew, shouting, "Put this on—we're all in this together!" But it wasn't my church so I let it pass. Now when the day comes that the material things of the church really belong to us and we participate in them, I suspect they will come to mean something to us (and also that we won't buy any more than we need). What if instead of hiring a custodian, all of the men of the church came regularly and did the yard work and the painting while the women cleaned the interior? (Don't start on me about the women's lib thing; you can do it the other way around if you want to.) What if we did our own cooking, our own painting, our own mimeographing, and our own plumbing? I'll bet it wouldn't be long until we started doing our own singing, and our own praying, and our own pastoral calling, just as though Christianity were something that was meant for all of us!

What I'm saying is that things are to be loved, respected, and cared for by the church, but not taken too seriously. In some ways, the model for us is the tabernacle of the Hebrew people in their wilderness wanderings. It had a lot going for it. The last six chapters of the book of Exodus give a detailed description of it and a number of things stand out. The tabernacle (the word

102

simply means "tent") really belonged to the people. It wasn't a gift to them from a missions committee; they didn't inherit it from their ancestors. No, they made it out of their own jewels and clothing (my, but they came away from Egypt with a lot of loot!) and pieced it together themselves with all the skill and devotion they could muster. True, it was in some ways luxurious, being made of gold, fine linens, and precious stones. It was the best they could offer. But it wasn't permanent! No, the building was "pre-fabricated;" it could be taken down on a moment's notice and moved to the next oasis as their wanderings continued. Even the furniture was portable (see chap. 37). All the main articles had rings attached to them through which poles could be thrust for easy carrying. (How movable is the altar in your church?) There was a certain freedom about it, as though the people who worshiped there did not think that they had permanently arrived at First Methodist Church on the Corner, but were on a pilgrimage, trusting God at any moment to pick them up and move them on to their next adverture.

What if we could so picture our own church's property: to be loved, cared for, and then, when the time comes, moved on? There is a security in great stone edifices but, for all its serenity, it can be a false security. If you ever get a chance to do so be sure to tour the magnificent Episcopal Cathedral of St. John the Divine in New York City. This is the largest Protestant edifice, I believe. But it is a cathedral with a difference. Within the cool stone magnificence of its Gothic beauty there are some remarkable happenings: music and dance workshops, programs for housing and rehabilitation of the poor, and other "nonchurch" activities. Indeed, it serves as a haven to some non-Christian bodies who have no other place to worship. The cathedral has been called "a holy place for the whole city." It is not afraid to go among the publicans and sinners doing good, as our Master taught by example. But perhaps best of all is the decision recently made by the leaders of the cathedral *not to finish the uncompleted portion* of the great building. Instead, they have elected to let it stand, the cement block contrasting with the Gothic stonework, as a perpetual reminder that God's work in the world is unfinished and that hunger and human misery have our first priority.

Or think also of the Coventry Cathedral in Great Britain, where, out of the ashes of the old ruins, like a phoenix, the new rises up. This also is a sign for us of the day that is coming when, out of the too, too insubstantial flesh of our world, God will erect a new and permanent building, "a house not made with hands, eternal in the heavens" (II Cor. 5:1).

X THE GATES

Now we are at the end, and where has it all led us? I hope that a part of you has been greatly frustrated by a theme that seems to be running throughout this book: namely, that the material world is really more than we can handle. It fills us with anxiety, selfishness, uncertainty, and sometimes lust. It leads us to hunger, over-population, inhumanity, and, in the long run, death. It is almost as though we were saying, "The world is too much with us," that we can't make it. I hope you have been feeling that, because I believe that to be the truth. It is summarized by Jesus in one of his funniest and, at the same time, most terrifying statements, in Mark 10:25: "It is easier for a camel to go through the eye of a needle than for a rich man to enter the kingdom of God." The disciples never forgot that one. Nor has anyone else who ever heard it. Partly this is due to the radically ridiculous image of a great big thousand-pound dromedary squeezing into a hole barely big enough to see (I can't thread one, even with my glasses on). But partly it is due to the news it contains: If you are wealthy, you can't get to ✓ heaven. Nobody wants to hear that.

There have been many attempts to weasel out of this harsh statement (I suppose it would be easier to weasel through a needle's eye than to camel it), but none of them will wash. It doesn't work to hypothesize a gate known as the Needle's Eye through which the camel *could* go, if he strained and stretched. Even if there is such a gate, it won't do. Jesus' words carry their own ominous reality. It is as sure a statement as morality knows: riches and righteousness, like drunkenness and driving, cannot mix. Why does it take so long to come to the conclusion that has been staring us in the face all the time? Maybe Jesus really meant what he said. Certainly that is what the disciples thought. When they heard this harsh news, they were taken aback. Mark 10:24-27 reports the conversation: "And they were exceedingly astonished, and said to him, 'Then who can be saved?'" That does not sound like those who are figuring out a riddle about a needle; that sounds like thoroughly frightened men who are looking at their own life-styles and recognizing that in their own way they are as rich as the next fellow.

They are saying, in effect, "Then salvation is impossible."

"Exactly," said Jesus. "With men it *is* impossible."

"Then," and this is my question and yours perhaps, as well as that of the disciples, "then I am lost?"

"Yes," answered Jesus. "You are. That is—except for one thing."

"And what is that?"

"It is a miracle: with men it is impossible, but not with God, for all things are possible with God."

Paul would have said, "By the works of your own hand you'll never do it, but by the gift of God, it is a reality." (see Eph. 2:8-9). In other words, there is no person on earth, no matter how poor and dejected, who is not, in the eyes of God, guilty of being rich in a world where sharing is the necessary ingredient. I know that sounds arrogant. I mean, what right have I, a member of the American middle class, to be telling the poor of Africa or Asia that they are rich? None whatsoever. Judgment is God's prerogative (Matt. 7:1). I can make no such pronouncement. But I must try to discern what reality I can. And to me, reality looks something like the following story. It was told to me by a used car salesman who talks like a theologian. (Some say that nobody in good conscience could *be* a used car salesman unless he *is* a theologian.)

> The human race is like tiny organisms that live in the narrow film of water on the surface of a cypress swamp. In that brief liquid millimeter they swim, trying to out do one another and reach a higher level, closer to the surface. In relation to each other, some of them seem very important, others insignificant. But to the eye of God who, in this fable is a bright white egret, sitting in the very top of a tall cypress, all the creatures of the bracken appear on the same level. The distinctions of rich and poor, slave and free, big and little, sick and well, righteous and unrighteous, all blend into one vast crowd of sinful humanity, of whom the scripture rightly says, "None is righteous, no, not one" (Rom. 3:10; see also Ps. 14:1-3).

That illustration, unfortunately, sounds like a put-down to all human effort, and some take offense at it; but I wonder if it is not close to the truth. Isn't it our basic human error to take our gnat-strivings too seriously? Do we not build towers to Babel or set out to rid the world of heretics (like Paul on the road to Damascus), only to find that our intense righteousness has all been for nonsense and that we are more blind or dumb than ever before? (Gen. 11:7; Acts 9:8-9).

Consider the following tale:

There were two grocery stores, one across the street from the other. The Acme Market was run by a dedicated Christian who was committed, both by personal faith and by vocation, to serving his fellow man in the most loving and useful way possible. At first, moved by good intentions, he tried selling his wares at ridiculously low prices so that the poor of the neighborhood could eat in relative comfort. But it soon dawned on him that if he did not charge high enough prices to be able to keep up his store, pay his help a decent wage, and keep his own children from starving, he would very quickly be out of business. So, before long, he found that he had to charge a modestly high price for all the groceries he sold.

On the other side of the street was the Ajax Market, run by a completely selfish man who was an avowed agnostic. He did not care a fig about community goodwill; all that mattered to him was that he turn a fast profit and be done with it. But he had not been in the business very long before he discovered that if he was to stay in business he had to keep his prices down at least low enough for people to come back the second time. In fact, he had to stay competitive with the Acme Market if he expected to survive economically.

The end result was this: if you were a complete stranger coming to that community, you might shop in either one of these grocery stores without being able to tell them apart! In each one you would find a genial proprietor, trying his best to keep the good will of his customers; in each one you would find relatively high prices, a modest profit, and a fairly nice collection of stock boys and check-out girls. In other words, you could not tell the difference between the players without a program.

Now, for what it is worth, that is the gospel of the New Testament; Don't take yourself too seriously! (I Cor. 3:18; Rom. 12:3). You are a part of the created world and none too important at that. If you wish to be first on the list, go to the foot of the table (Luke 14:7-11). If you want to be greatest in the kingdom of God, and to sit on the right hand of Jesus in the great day, you will have to become as a little child (Luke 9:46-50). There is no escaping the inexorable logic: if you expect to go home, it will have to be by way of the cross.

This means that there will be no earthly rewards for your Christian attitude toward the material world. On the contrary, you may be laughed out of court by half of the world for your ridiculous views, and outdistanced by the rest for not going far enough. This happened to Jesus. There were those who called John the Baptist crazy because he was an ascetic, and at the same time called Jesus immoral because he enjoyed life (Matt. 11:18-19)! "You are like children," Jesus implied. "Whatever game we're playing, you want to play another one!" Or, as in Matthew 11:17, "We piped to you, and you did not dance; We wailed, and you did not mourn." Instead of being child-*like,* the world is child-*ish.* The human race is riding on a merry-go-round, grabbing for the brass ring, and paying little or no attention to where they are going. We snatch like a spoiled child for that which our playmates have, and whine when we do not get the biggest piece. In that sort of world, the Christian easily may be the innocent victim. He's like the child in the story who said, "You're greedy! A polite person would have taken the smaller piece." "Would you have taken it," asked his playmate. "Certainly. I'm a Christian." "Well, then, what are you complaining about? You got what you wanted." If you act like a Christian, you may get stepped on.

But that isn't the worst thing that can happen to you. On the contrary, Jesus said, "Blessed are you when men revile you and persecute you and utter all kinds of evil against you falsely on my account. Rejoice and be glad, for your reward is great in heaven" (Matt. 5:11-12). The worst thing that could happen would be to fall into the trap of believing that the world is your oyster, and that life was meant for looking out for number one and getting rich quick. Those who act that way may seem on the surface to live fat and happy lives. As the psalmist said: "They are not in trouble as other men are" (Ps. 73:5). But they are! He who puts his faith in the world of things is worshiping an idol which will, in the end, be his undoing. In the sanctuary of God the psalmist saw the truth: "Then I perceived their end. Truly thou dost set them in slippery places; thou dost make them fall to ruin" (Ps. 73:17-18). And when the natural world turns on us, that is, when the rain falls and the flood comes and the wind blows and beats against the house, woe unto him who has not built on the true foundation of obedience to the Lord of the world (Matt. 7:24-27)!

So we won't be popular when we advocate love for nature, care for things, wonder at life, generosity in sharing, and stewardship for coming generations. But that is no matter. Popularity is not why we're in the game. We're in the game because we want to be on the right side and we're going to win. That is something that we'll have to handle on faith, but it is that faith which will make the kingdom possible: "And I tell you, you are my Peter, and on this rock will I build my church, and the powers of death shall not prevail against it" (Matt. 16:18). I think we have a tendency to think of the church a standing its ground against the attack of the forces of darkness. But in Jesus' words, it is not the church that is under attack, it is the gates of hell! It is we who are to do the storming! When we picture the church with *its* gates closed, we tend to build ivory towers, material bastions, cathedrals that hold men and women in subjection to institutions, building programs, and the preservation of *things*. But we were meant to be a free people, nomads of the road, going with Jesus from village to village doing battle against the powers of evil. It is the gates of hell that are on the defensive, trembling in fear. They cannot take the material world from us; it belongs to the human race by the gift of God in creation, and we will use it to do battle. And we are going to win.

The gates of the church are never closed (see Rev. 21:25). In the heat of the battle, in the gloom of the world's night, the bright light streams forth from the open doors of the city where grow the leaves for the healing of the nations. Its doors do not need to be closed, for all souls who will come are welcome there. Nothing unclean can enter; God has written that in his book. We do not have to defend *that* gate. Rather, we are free to venture forth into the world to storm the gates of hell, and with our Lord to rescue the weary creation which is crushed under the load of man's inhumanity. We are free indeed, if the Son has made us free—free to touch, taste, hear, and see all the varied wavelengths of the spectrum of his world. As e. e. cummings sang: "i who have died am alive again today." To those who believe in God, the world becomes a laboratory for discovery, a source of growth and hope, and a promise of a new world to come. To those who long, like the young deer for the stream,

after his way and his law, the promise of Isaiah 55
already is dawning:

Ho, every one who thirsts,
   come to the waters;
and he who has no money,
   come, buy and eat!
Come, buy wine and milk
   without money and without price.
Why do you spend your money for that which is not
    bread,
   and your labor for that which does not satisfy?

Seek the Lord while he may be found,
   call upon him while he is near;
let the wicked forsake his way,
   and the unrighteous man his thoughts;
let him return to the Lord,
   that he may have mercy on him,
and to our God, for he will abundantly pardon.

For as the rain and the snow come down from heaven,
   and return not thither but water the earth,
making it bring forth and sprout,
   giving seed to the sower and bread to the eater,
so shall my word be that goes forth from my mouth;
   it shall not return to me empty,
but it shall accomplish that which I purpose,
   and prosper in the thing for which I sent it.

For you shall go out in joy,
   and be led forth in peace;
the mountains and the hills before you
   shall break forth into singing,
   and all the trees of the field shall clap their hands.